Complete Conditioning for
VOLLEYBALL

Al Scates
Head Volleyball Coach
UCLA

Mike Linn
Strength and Conditioning Coach
Saint Louis University

with
Vince Kowalick

Library of Congress Cataloging-in-Publication Data

Scates, Allen E.
  Complete conditioning for volleyball / Al Scates, Michael Linn.
    p. cm.
  ISBN 0-7360-0136-0 (softcover)
  1. Volleyball—Training. I. Linn, Michael, 1969- II. Title.
  GV1015.5.T73 S23 2003
  796.325—dc21   2002013753

ISBN: 0-7360-0136-0

Production Editor: Melinda Graham; **Assistant Editor:** John Wentworth; **Copyeditor:** KLM Words; **Proofreader:** Erin Cler; **Permission Manager:** Toni Harte; **Graphic Designer:** Stuart Cartwright; **Art and Photo Manager:** Dan Wendt; **Cover Designer:** Jack W. Davis; **Photographer (cover):** Scott Quintard/UCLA Photography; **Photographers (interior):** Tom Roberts unless otherwise noted; Scott Quintard/UCLA Photography pages 9, 10, 132, and 202; Don Liebig page 57; Peter Brouillet pages 12 and 18; Getty Images, page 84; ©Tony Duffy/The Sporting Image, pages 4, 40, and 59; and © Robert Tringali/SportsChrome, page 82; ASUCLA Athletics, page 203; Saint Louis University, page 203; **Illustrator:** Brian McElwain; **Printer:** Custom Color Graphics

Human Kinetics books are available at special discounts for bulk purchase. Special editions or book excerpts can also be created to specification. For details, contact the Special Sales Manager at Human Kinetics.

Printed in the United States of America

10 9 8 7 6 5 4 3 2 1

Human Kinetics
Web site: www.HumanKinetics.com

United States: Human Kinetics
P.O. Box 5076
Champaign, IL 61825-5076
800-747-4457
e-mail: humank@hkusa.com

Canada: Human Kinetics
475 Devonshire Road Unit 100
Windsor, ON N8Y 2L5
800-465-7301 (in Canada only)
e-mail: orders@hkcanada.com

Europe: Human Kinetics
107 Bradford Road
Stanningley
Leeds LS28 6AT, United Kingdom
+44 (0) 113 255 5665
e-mail: hk@hkeurope.com

Australia: Human Kinetics
57A Price Avenue
Lower Mitcham, South Australia 5062
08 8277 1555
e-mail: liahka@senet.com.au

New Zealand: Human Kinetics
P.O. Box 105-231, Auckland Central
09-523-3462
e-mail: hkp@ihug.co.nz

CONTENTS

FOREWORD

At the risk of stating the utterly obvious, Coach Scates has been the preeminent coach in American volleyball for over 30 years now. No other coach has guided teams to excellence so often and so consistently. So whenever he says anything about volleyball, I listen carefully and take notes—I started with his first literary effort *Winning Volleyball* (Allyn & Bacon, 1972), which I borrowed from my dad and never gave back. It still sits on my volleyball bookshelf today. Now it is time for all of us to whip out our notepads again, because Al's giving another clinic on how he has kept his teams on top for so long.

First, as Coach Scates says, his program has to worry about survival each year. One of the unintended consequences of Title IX is that men's collegiate sports besides football and basketball are fighting for their lives. UCLA, the most successful collegiate athletic department in the country, has dropped men's gymnastics, swimming, and water polo, among others, due to Title IX and budgetary constraints. That leaves UCLA men's volleyball scrambling to justify its existence each and every year, and it leaves me amazed at how someone can become the winningest coach of all time in an environment like that.

After reading about how willing Coach Scates is to adapt, to try new concepts, to make drastic changes, even to rework the program, I understand better how he's achieved success in every era of a game that has evolved so radically over the last three decades: the six-hitter two-setter era, and the five-hitter one-setter era too; using no backcourt hitting, or using a lot; pre libero, post-libero; playing with sideout scoring, or with rally-point scoring; with old-time short players or ever-growing tall ones. The four teams I had the good fortune to play on achieved such success—we had a record of 124-5—and required so much less tinkering, that I didn't realize how much Coach Scates is willing to embrace change when necessary.

From my first day in practice, I learned that everything Al does, and everything his teams do, is focused on becoming a better team than the one on the other side of the net. Every volleyball drill, every conditioning drill, and every strength drill had a clear purpose, accomplishing its task efficiently. For example, Al inculcated in me, and most of his players, an absolute loathing of any spiking drill that allows hitters to attack on an open net—that is, an attacking drill with no blockers offering resistance on the other side of the net. I'll never forget all the times I walked through Pauley Pavilion after practicing in the men's gym, watching the women hit ball after ball with no live set and no live block, scratching my head and thinking, "When will *that* ever happen in a game?"

The things that don't work one year are filed away, maybe never to be used again, while Coach Scates finds a new way to win the next year. That allows him to have run just about every drill, every idea through the testing sieve, and what's left, what really works, can be found in this book—which is why I shouldn't be surprised at how few of the drills look familiar to me.

I wish I'd had the opportunity to read this book before I entered UCLA, instead of over 20 years later—it would have prepared me better for the battles we had in practice every day, and for how Al allows no sacred cows, gives nobody a guaranteed spot on the court. I was shocked my freshman year when Joe Mica—who had been an NCAA All-Tournament selection twice and an NCAA Tournament MVP once in previous seasons—sat on the bench most of his senior year. But Coach Scates knew exactly what he was doing, as he explains here, forcing every player to compete for his position every day. So Mica was properly prepared to lead us to victory when Al substituted him into the title match (and he earned another All-Tournament selection to boot). That is only one of many episodes where Al has pulled a rabbit out of his hat.

So here you have a treasure trove of ideas on how to improve yourself as a player or improve your team as a coach. I wish you well in your attempt to put them to use. Coach Scates says, "With winning comes a mystery." I hope you enjoy listening to him unravel the mystery as much as I have.

Karch Kiraly

ACKNOWLEDGMENTS

Thanks to Paula Weishoff, one of the all world great middle blockers who shared her dedication to training with us.

Special thanks to Hall of Famer Patty Dowdell, who told us how she stayed at the top of her game. This has been going on for three decades, from the USA Team in the 1970s through a USA Open MVP Award in the 1990s.

I want to thank Coach Russ Rose for his interesting story about Christy Cochran. Russ has spent 23 seasons as the Head Women's Coach at Penn State and his .846 winning percentage ranks number one nationally.

TRAIN TO BE A CHAMPION

The UCLA men's volleyball team has enjoyed tremendous success over the years. Maintaining a winning environment hasn't been easy, however. Forced to contend with many rapidly improving college programs each season, we are forced each year to begin anew and rededicate ourselves. Many variables are involved, including new recruits, injuries, and graduation; and achieving success with each is crucial. To contend with stronger competition, we must recondition ourselves each season. Fortunately, the Bruins have usually been able to be in the peak of condition when the NCAA playoffs begin. That's because the players have prepared well in advance. Our athletes are well aware of the importance of dedicating themselves to a rigorous conditioning program throughout the year. They experience firsthand the fruits of their labor with the rewards of championship, often won by the narrowest of margins. In the final analysis, the difference between success and failure might come down to conditioning.

The Bruins have won 18 NCAA men's volleyball championships over the past 33 years. Four times, they have finished second in the finals.

Why the success? Every year brings a renewed and dedicated commitment to win. By committing to working harder than our opponents, our players invest in the program. They believe that because of superior conditioning we have an advantage in the fifth game of any match.

I ask myself the following questions annually: What are my goals? What are the team's weaknesses and strengths? What should we look for in recruiting players? What do I expect from my players and assistant coaches?

Naturally, it is a group effort undertaken by a collection of highly dedicated people willing to work hard and make sacrifices. As coach of UCLA for 40 seasons, I have relied on several qualities of leadership I believe are most important.

- Intelligence. I surround myself with intelligent coaches who can identify and recruit talented and self-motivated players who will thrive in our competitive program.

- Passion. I look for players who live, breathe, and dream about the same goals I have.

- Fearlessness. I am willing to make drastic changes to achieve my goals. This includes personnel and tactical changes.

- Vision. I do whatever it takes to win within the rules. If I think the sport can be improved, I lobby hard for rule changes.

It's all a matter of molding raw materials into a winning combination. At practice, the atmosphere is loose and relaxed during warm-ups, but once I enter the gym, I want the tension to heighten and the players to get serious. Practices are more intense than games because each player is constantly fighting to maintain his right to be on the court. Practices are simulations of games, and when the second team wins a drill, it is lauded as a victory. If the second team is not strong, the first team rarely achieves its potential. I watch the first team and frequently interject commands. I talk frequently with the setter, the way a football coach confers with his quarterback, and I expect him to follow directions.

A team, by its very nature, has a hierarchical order: a head coach, a first and second assistant, and a volunteer coach. The first team plays in the most important games. The second team provides competition for the first team during practice, and members of the second team rotate into the first team on an as-needed basis.

My first assistant has been coaching at UCLA for 12 seasons. He lettered at UCLA three years as a middle blocker and was a member of our first undefeated team in 1979. Brian Rofer was never a starter in our program but was a valuable contributor who knows the type of player we need to win an NCAA championship. Brian is in charge of recruiting and scouting, and he works with me on the first court.

My second assistant was a four-year letterman who set our 1993 team to a 24-3 season and our 14th NCAA championship. We hit .420 that season, which is the current NCAA record. Mike Sealy has played professionally in Europe since then and is now embarking on a coaching career with UCLA. Mike is in charge of the second court and is developing players for next season. In addition, he monitors our student-athletes' academic progress and helps with scouting.

Our volunteer assistant coach is Jeff Nygaard, UCLA's player of the year in 1994 and 1995, and a member of the U.S. Olympic team in 1996 and 2000.

Only players whom I have coached for four or five years are employed as my assistants. This ensures that they well understand the competitive structure I create for players.

Practices are competitive in nature, with players moving from the first team to the second team and from the second court to the first. If the first team loses a drill, usually a player from the second team moves up to replace a starter. If the second team is not competitive, a player typically will move to the second court with a corresponding player moving up.

The squad suiting up for the next match is not announced until after the last practice, and changes often are made from the last match based on the performance in recent practices. All coaches are encouraged to give immediate feedback to players without disrupting the flow of drills.

Because this is a competitive sport team, winning is the only measure of success. At UCLA, winning the NCAA championship every year is our goal. Our history of success demands a higher level of expectation than that of any other team in the country. Those expectations are met through a serious commitment to conditioning.

I look at statistics, develop practice and game plans, scrutinize video of matches, and travel around the world with the U.S. men's volleyball team. My assistants help with coaching during practice, recruiting new players, and serving as academic counselors to the student-athletes. Team captains usually are chosen by the players.

After each season I meet with our weight coach and discuss specific technical problems the returning players may have. We explore whether there are any strength exercises that we need to use to help them attain proficiency in the specific technique. For example, two of my best middle blockers did not have an explosive, long first step to get to the outside last season. If the weight coach has a solution to this problem, he adds it to the summer weight conditioning manual so that the athlete develops the strength to execute the step in the fall.

The team's success depends on each person's ability to develop his personal responsibilities. We give each player much individual responsibility, and each is asked to develop his own level of maturity based on his commitment. The program is strict, but we foster the spirit of competitiveness by allowing each player to develop his own drive. Those who respond to this call for maturity excel in the program. Some players who started on championship teams for UCLA waited four years to become starters.

Many high school players are not physically strong enough to compete at the college level in their first season. We put these players on a strong, three-day-a-week conditioning program and redshirt them. They train with the team but save a year of eligibility. After one year they jump higher, move more quickly, and become better players.

We convey the responsibility of winning to each team. Each member joins in the enormous responsibility of maintaining a legacy. Because of UCLA's success, many programs regard the Bruins as the standard to match or overcome. When a team consistently wins, it becomes the focus of every opponent. We must constantly adjust each season to maintain the winning tradition.

Our season is finished the first weekend in May, and we do not start training together as a team until October. Players who do not live near campus are responsible for weight training on their own by following the summer conditioning manual provided by our strength coach. Players who live near campus continue to train with our strength coach. Players who are not willing to train on their own during breaks risk falling behind on the depth chart and rarely become starters.

Every year it is a struggle to stay on top. The job requires constant monitoring and the ability to combine multiple resources. Even the most talented coach, however, cannot succeed without players who work to become superbly conditioned.

CHAPTER 1

VOLLEYBALL PERFORMANCE FACTORS

The popularity of volleyball has grown in leaps and bounds in the past two decades, and the game continues to build momentum at the professional, collegiate, and scholastic levels. Long considered more pastime than sport, the game's appeal in the United States skyrocketed after the U.S. men's team won Olympic gold medals in 1984 and 1988. The sport has since earned its niche in the American sports landscape for the same reason other popular sports have: raw power and athleticism.

The pace of the game has quickened since 1964, when it was introduced as an Olympic sport. In those days players seldom dove to the floor, and strategy involved few of the intricate combinations of setters and hitters used in today's game. Today, a typical rally in a men's or women's collegiate game lasts only about 10 to 15 seconds. Rules have changed, too. Players are allowed to block over the net, placing a greater emphasis on the vertical aspect of the game. These changes have contributed to a need for greater conditioning among players. In fact, it often proves to be the deciding factor.

In 1996, perennial power UCLA faced a fired-up Hawaii team determined to deny the Bruins a second consecutive national title in the NCAA men's championship at Pauley Pavilion. Led by outside hitter Yuval Katz, who registered 47 kills and eventually was selected the tournament's most valuable player, Hawaii took a 2-1 lead in games and held a 9-7 lead in the fifth and deciding game at Pauley.

Yet Katz was less effective down the stretch, while UCLA's Paul Nihipali shook off fatigue that escalated during the 3-hour, 11-minute match and made the more defining plays. Nihipali twice stuffed Katz in the deciding game while recording six kills to lead the Bruins to a 15-12 victory and their 16th NCAA title. "I thought we had our chance once we caught them in the fourth game," Hawaii coach Mike Wilton said after the match. "But we didn't seem to make the plays we needed to at the end."

In the end, the difference was the exceptional condition of the UCLA players, who committed to rigorous training throughout the season and during the off-season. Simply recruiting the nation's top players won't result in success. The Bruins' 20 national championships under coach Al Scates are a testimony to an attitude toward the team's conditioning more than anything else. Over the years, UCLA players have come to realize that the longer a match goes, the greater their chances of winning. Why? They're in optimum volleyball shape.

Today, players must be able to move, jump, and swing with power and speed regardless of their sizes and positions. Top-level players today are quicker, stronger, and in better physical condition than ever before—not because of evolution but because they have followed the lead of other high-level athletes by training year-round and developing techniques that add strength, power, and fitness specific to their sport.

To be exceptional volleyball players today, athletes not only must be in excellent shape, they must be in volleyball shape. What is volleyball shape? A player who has a 35-inch vertical leaping ability and can run for miles without tiring won't necessarily be a good volleyball player, just as training for a marathon won't necessarily improve a runner's performance in sprints. Volleyball players must be able to jump to the same height near the end of a long and grueling match as at the beginning. They must have the energy to perform physical feats while sustaining their levels of strength, power, and agility. Moreover, players must condition themselves to combat against injuries common to volleyball—most notably *jumper's knee*, which eventually affects all players to a certain degree.

How do we decide what types of strength, power, flexibility, and agility are important to volleyball and what is the best way to go about conditioning? First, we must understand the physiological and biomechanical needs of volleyball players.

Karch Kiraly and Sinjin Smith

Karch Kiraly (143) and Sinjin Smith (139) rank number 1 and number 2 in professional beach volleyball tournament victories. When Smith was a senior captain at UCLA, Kiraly was an incoming freshman. Smith was a great team leader who immediately recognized Kiraly's potential and paired with him for team drills and strength exercises. In those days there was no rally scoring, and five-game matches could last up to three and a half hours. The UCLA team usually was in better shape than its opponent, thanks to a daily strenuous conditioning program that incorporated 300 push-ups and 300 sit-ups with short sprints, dives, ball handling, and jumps before beginning court drills.

Kiraly and Smith competed against each other on a daily basis in every exercise. They competed to see who could complete the push-ups and sit-ups first, who could sprint the fastest and jump the highest. Their pepper games were extraordinary because of the speed of their spikes and great defensive reactions. When they came to practice, they concentrated solely on volleyball. No surprise that both players are in the UCLA Hall of Fame and had their jersey numbers retired.

In June 2002, Kiraly at 41 became the oldest player to win an Association of Volleyball Professionals tournament, extending his record for career victories. He has three Olympic gold medals and is a member of the Volleyball Hall of Fame.

ENERGY SYSTEMS

When designing any workout program it is important to recognize the athlete's need for energy. All sports rely on some type of energy system. Some share the same basic needs, while others are completely different (see table 1.1). To understand a volleyball player's energy needs, we must understand the body's energy systems and how they are trained.

Training can be divided into aerobic and anaerobic activities. *Aerobic* means *with oxygen,* and *anaerobic* means *without oxygen.* Activities such as running marathons and cross-country skiing have a long duration and low power output. They involve the intake of lots of oxygen, requiring energy from aerobic sources. By contrast, activities with short duration and high power output require less oxygen and therefore require anaerobic sources of energy. Volleyball falls into the latter category. Matches are long, but play is not continuous. With many breaks in the action, demand for oxygen is less than it is in other sports. The power output needed during the 10 to 15 seconds of a rally, however, is extremely high. The high power output is provided by anaerobic energy.

The two sources of anaerobic energy are the phosphagen system and the glycogen-lactic acid system. The phosphagen system provides the high-energy compound adenosine triphosphate (ATP), which is readily available to muscle. Activities that require high power output, such as the

The dive requires a high power output.

Table 1.1 Primary Metabolic Demands of Various Sports

Sport	Phosphagen system	Anaerobic glycolysis	Aerobic metabolism
Baseball	high	low	—
Basketball	high	moderate to high	—
Diving	high	low	—
Field events	high	—	—
Field hockey	high	moderate	moderate
Football	high	moderate	low
Gymnastics	high	moderate	—
Golf	high	—	—
Ice hockey	high	moderate	moderate
Lacrosse	high	moderate	moderate
Soccer	high	moderate	high
Swimming, sprint	high	moderate to high	—
Swimming, distance	high	moderate to high	—
Tennis	high	—	—
Track, sprint	high	moderate to high	—
Track, distance	—	moderate	high
Volleyball	high	moderate	—

Note: All types of metabolism are involved to some extent in all activities. Only primary or near primary metabolic systems for each are shown in this table.

quick, explosive jumps in volleyball, rely heavily on ATP. The glycogen-lactic acid system involves glycolysis, the breakdown of glucose to lactic acid. Activities that require multiple bursts of power for an extended period depend on the breakdown of glucose for energy. Table 1.2 shows the relationship between energy systems and exercise duration.

Next, we need to determine how to train these energy systems. ATP, which uses the substance creatine phosphate, can be increased only through training bouts that elicit high power output and, in turn, produce larger gains in the muscles' phosphagen content. Movements such as Olympic lifts and squats are the best methods of achieving this, and they make up the bulk of our weight training program devoted to developing strength and power. In conditioning, short-distance sprints and agility drills that fall into the proper work-to-rest ratio are best for training energy systems. Determining how to prescribe the right volume, intensity, and load of these exercises throughout the year is part of developing a year-round conditioning program.

Table 1.2 Effect of Event Duration on Primary Energy System Used

Duration of event	Intensity of event	Primary energy system(s)
0-6 seconds	very intense	Phosphagen
6-30 seconds	intense	Phosphagen and fast glycolysis
30 seconds- 2 minutes	heavy	Fast glycolysis
2-3 minutes	moderate	Fast glycolysis and oxidative system
>3 minutes	light	Oxidative system

BIOMECHANICAL NEEDS

Every sport also has its own mechanical needs. Proper training for one sport isn't necessarily the proper method for another because of differing physical demands. When a volleyball player jumps and spikes the ball over the net, a variety of physical movements combine during that split second of power. The player must plant the feet; bring the body under control; flex the ankles, knees, and hips; and then extend them all in succession before reacting to the ball in flight by extending the triceps and forearm, and violently transferring all that energy through the ball. This succession of movements can be simplified into two basic aspects of volleyball: the jump and the swing.

Jeff Nygaard

Jeff Nygaard has achieved legendary status among UCLA recruits because of his emergence from seemingly nowhere to become one of the Bruins best players.

Nygaard, a lanky 17-year-old high school player, was "discovered" on a high school recruiting videotape that featured him proudly pointing to his high school championship banner. Nygaard, 6 feet, 7 inches and 160 pounds, spent his freshman year in 1992 redshirting for the Bruins while working on the second court with fellow redshirts John Speraw, Eric Sullivan, and Kevin Wong. At that time, UCLA had only one full-time weight coach and one assistant for all sports. Nygaard was given a program and lifted weights on his own. With no team weightlifting program at the time, the Bruins' strength training had varied results, depending on the diligence of each athlete.

Nygaard embraced training and did not miss a workout. He faithfully documented his lifts and recorded amazing gains in strength in a short time. By the end of his first season he weighed 190 pounds, gaining 25 pounds of muscle. Nygaard was a starter the next four seasons, contributing to three NCAA championships and one second-place finish. By the time he left UCLA, Nygaard was much stronger than when he had arrived and 50 pounds heavier. He joined the USA team, playing in two Olympics before signing on as a volunteer coach. During this time, Nygaard followed the UCLA weight training program. He increased his workout regimen to four times a week while preparing for the Association of Volleyball Professionals (AVP) beach tour. Once the tour began, Nygaard reduced his regimen to three times a week and soon won his first AVP event.

Today, Nygaard weighs 220 pounds with very little body fat. With a great training program and outstanding blocking technique, he is certain to have success in his new career as a pro beach volleyball player.

The Jump

The major muscles used in the jump are the glutes, hamstrings, quadriceps, and calves. These muscles are attached to the joints of the lower extremities and work together to generate the power needed to get off the ground. The major joints used are the ankle, knee, and hip. With the aid of muscles, these joints work in unison to perform what is called *triple extension*. Before the jump, the athlete gets into what is called *triple flexion*, flexing the knees, ankles, and hips. This places the athlete in a ready position from which to generate maximum power. From there, the athlete explosively extends all three joints to get the body off the ground.

By understanding which muscles and joints are used in the jump, we can determine which exercises are best for training. The jump is known as a *closed-chain* activity, meaning an exercise in which the exercising segment of the body is attached to a fixed surface (the floor), requiring the entire limb (the legs) to bear resistance. In this case, the resistance is the player's weight fighting gravity to get off the ground. The opposite of a closed-chain activity is an exercise in which the end of the exercising body segment does not touch a fixed surface. Squats are an example of a closed-chain activity, and they are the primary exercise used in leg strength training. Leg curls and leg extensions are examples of *open-chain* activities.

The Olympic lifts—power cleans, power snatches, and their complementary exercises—incorporate both triple extension and closed-chain activities and are the best examples of sport-specific training for the jump.

While the combination of triple extension and closed-chain activities is also present in other sports, it is often overlooked during training off the court. Remember, the key is being sport specific. If the bulk of your leg work comes from open-chain exercises that don't involve simultaneous triple extension, you are wasting valuable time in training.

The Swing

Getting players to swing faster boils down to a lot of basic technique and fundamentals. Generally, the player with the faster swing at impact will hit the ball harder. Upper-body strength, stability of the shoulder socket, and functional trunk strength will allow a player to swing faster and more powerfully. As in the jump, the key is extension. The player who extends the shoulder and elbow with the most speed and power will hit the ball harder and faster. Elbow extension accounts for about half of the

Explosive jumpers like Danny Farmer often hit before the block is formed.

power output, followed by shoulder rotation and torso rotation. With this knowledge, we can assign exercises to promote strength gains in each of these areas.

Full elbow extension is one of the keys to hitting the ball harder and faster.

IMPORTANT ATTRIBUTES

To achieve volleyball-specific shape, a well-conditioned athlete must develop attributes, including flexibility, strength, power, and agility. Although that may seem obvious, it is the type of flexibility and the type of strength that determine whether a player is in volleyball shape. The flexibility needs of volleyball players differ from those of soccer players or swimmers. Their aspects of strength are different from those of football players, baseball players, or distance runners. The type of agility that must be developed is unlike that required in any other sport.

Like basketball players, volleyball athletes must be able to leap with agility and power—but they also need to be able to hit a nine-ounce volleyball with a thunderous force while suspended in midair. They must be able to leap to the net and block a spike that travels as fast as 100 miles per hour. They must go from leaping to diving to the floor in a matter of seconds. They must be able to react immediately and constantly throughout a two-hour match in a manner unique to the sport.

Because volleyball players' fitness needs differ from those of other athletes, they must train differently from other athletes. Volleyball has its own unique training puzzle that combines these variables. Following is an overview of the keys to achieving volleyball shape.

Flexibility

It is widely accepted that the more flexible athletes are, the less likely they are to become injured. Moreover, a player with great flexibility usually possesses great agility, strength, and power. Developing optimum range of motion in a specific joint and its surrounding muscles is especially imperative for volleyball players because they must be able to perform while constantly finding themselves in awkward positions during a match. The greater range of motion players have, the more easily their bodies can get into some of the awkward and unusual positions the game requires.

Strength

Strength is the maximum force that can be applied by a muscle or group of muscles to perform a given task. A nine-ounce volleyball delivered by a powerful swing can reach speeds of up to 100 miles per hour. Good blockers have the strength to block the ball at the net without allowing their arms or hands to move backward. The players who have the greater strength are the ones who will win the jousts at the net, forcing balls through opponents' hands and keeping balls from being forced through their own. Leg strength is equally important. It accounts for the ability to make the split-second changes in direction required of players. With good leg strength comes a greater potential for all-around power.

Power

Power is the amount of time and the amount of force a player uses to perform a given task within a fraction of a second. A powerful player has greater velocity to the arm swing, thus hitting the ball harder than other players. Power also relates to the ability to jump from the ground faster and ascend higher than other players. Players must explode from the floor, spending as little time as possible on the floor to maximize the height of a jump.

Power hitter.

Agility

Volleyball players must be able to change direction in a split second while maintaining control and balance, and they must be able to react immediately to a coming spike. They must position themselves instantly to make a block. They must be able to change direction in midair to adjust to the flight of the ball. Moreover, movements are specific to certain players. For instance, middle blockers must be able to jump up to 300 times in a five-game match, exploding off the floor to combat opposing hitters and then making the transition to aid in the attack from their team's side of the net.

Developing the performance factors—flexibility, strength, power, and agility—is the cornerstone of a well-devised conditioning program for volleyball players, but it accounts for only part of the equation. As the remaining chapters will discuss, an athlete's year-round dedication to the training regimen, which includes implementing a program of proper nutrition, is the ultimate deciding factor. This book provides solid, usable information. It is up to the athlete to apply it to life.

CHAPTER 2

FLEXIBILITY TRAINING

Coaches and athletes have long understood the importance of flexibility, yet all too often it is underemphasized and even overlooked. Too many athletes begin training without properly stretching and warming up their muscles. Some even forego the exercises entirely. Experienced coaches realize that athletes left to stretch on their own typically do a poor job—hence the need for stretching exercises during practice. To achieve maximum benefit from stretching, athletes need to stretch properly.

With stretching exercises, athletes must understand two important concepts: injury prevention and performance enhancement. The more flexible a muscle becomes, the less likely it is to be injured. And more flexible muscles, tendons, and ligaments translate into greater range of motion. By training through a greater range of motion, an athlete can recruit more muscle fibers, which leads to greater gains in power and agility.

During one season, one of UCLA's leading blockers felt tightness in his knee during a match and decided to perform a ballistic full squat to loosen up between games. He tore his medial meniscus, patellar tendon, and quadriceps tendon all in one thoughtless movement. That contributed to the Bruins' elimination in the first round of the playoffs. That athlete learned the hard way about the importance of proper stretching.

Flexibility as it pertains to volleyball is achieved through a combination of two basic types of stretching: stability stretching and mobility stretching. Although there are other types of stretching exercises, this chapter focuses on these two methods and how their combination is meant to provide optimum benefit for volleyball athletes in a shorter time.

STATIC STRETCHING

Static stretching is the most common of all stretching techniques, the one most athletes have been exposed to. It involves holding an individual stretch for a given time for the benefit of loosening up a specific muscle. Static stretches are not necessarily specific to a sport—that is, they include exercises that athletes typically perform as part of their general warm-up and are not designed to enhance performance in a specific manner. When performing stability stretches, it is important to follow some common rules. First, make sure you have the proper amount of space to perform the stretches properly. That will vary according to each person. Hold each stretch for between 20 and 30 seconds. Do not bounce. Ease into the stretch. Focus on breathing. Keep track of your flexibility from workout to workout, and record your progress. Concentrate on what you are doing. Don't let your mind wander.

DYNAMIC STRETCHING/WARM UP

Dynamic stretching involves movement while stretching and is more sport specific. These stretching exercises take an athlete's body through slow and controlled ranges of motion that apply to a specific sport. For example, a baseball pitcher performs physical tasks much different from those of a soccer player. Therefore, mobility stretches designed for the two athletes will differ. In the case of volleyball players, mobility stretching involves exercises that mirror physical tasks performed regularly during a match. As with stability stretches, be sure you have the proper amount of space to perform the stretches correctly. Perform each

Patty Dowdell

Early in Patty Dowdell's playing career, an elaborate approach to conditioning wasn't emphasized nearly as much as it is today. In fact, if it wasn't done on the court, it probably wasn't done.

"We hardly ever met in the weight room," recalls Dowdell, an All-American and member of the 1980 U.S. Olympic team forced to boycott the summer games in Moscow. "We would spend four to eight hours in the gym every day. We'd do [court] drills for four hours, sit-ups and push-ups and agility drills 'til the cows came home."

These days, Dowdell presides over a diverse conditioning program at Texas Woman's University, a Division II school in Dallas where she has served as head coach since 1996. The information is culled from a lengthy and illustrious career that included professional playing stints in Europe and the United States as well as coaching positions at three universities.

Dowdell's playing career peaked in 1994 when her club team won its fourth consecutive U.S. Volleyball Open championship and she garnered MVP honors. That year, she was elected to the Volleyball Hall of Fame. Dowdell is entering her seventh season at TWU after coaching at Iowa and De Pauw University in Greencastle, Indiana.

"It was all about how much hard work you put into it," Dowdell says. "Where we lacked in skill development and game experience, we made up for it in out-hustling the other team. I was always determined to do whatever it took to be the best. It was always how much I put into it that I got out of it. One more sit-up. One more rep with the weights."

Perhaps ahead of her time, Dowdell, a strength and conditioning specialist, at an early age developed a dedication to conditioning that separated her from many of her contemporaries. She emphasizes as much with today's players—though some struggle to fully appreciate the importance of even the simplest things. Like stretching.

"Stretching isn't popular among young players," Dowdell says. "The conception is that it's boring. We stretch after practice. It's a good time to work on hamstrings. But you have to remind them not to count too fast. You have to establish a routine."

exercise with control. Concentrate on the coaching points. Keep your power zone (abdominals and lower back) stable.

Performed separately, stability and mobility stretching are good ways to go about improving flexibility in general. But when incorporated together and performed properly in a well-devised program, the two methods can result in tremendous flexibility. That is why we choose both for this program.

Of course, as with all stretching exercises, athletes must take precautions to avoid injury. Coaches or a conditioning expert must monitor exercises, especially when athletes perform them for the first time. Each athlete should perform stretches according to individual flexibility and not to the expectations of others. This is particularly important when athletes stretch together as a group. When doing so, do not be concerned with how well your neighbor can stretch. Focus on your own limitations.

Flexible players can dig low balls.

Both forms of stretching are to be performed before training. This chapter will show the step-by-step progression desired. It also is important to stretch after games and practices. Studies have proven that stretching after a vigorous workout is effective in alleviating next-day soreness or injury. Only stability stretching, however, should be performed during the postworkout cool-down period.

WARMING UP

Now that we have established the basic forms of stretching, it's time to get started. First, before starting any type of stretching or physical activity, you need to warm up. Simple activities, like running a few laps around the court or riding a stationary bicycle, are good ways to get the blood pumping and the joints awakened. Your warm-up doesn't have to be complex. Generally, warm up for no longer than five minutes. A good warm-up provides several benefits:

- Increased blood flow to the muscles
- Elevated body temperature
- Awakened nervous system
- Mental preparedness for upcoming tasks

After properly warming up, perform the stretches. Remember the precautions and key concepts: injury prevention and performance enhancement. Above all, don't overdo it.

STATIC STRETCHES

STANDING V STRETCH

Purpose: To improve flexibility of hamstrings.

Procedure: Stand with legs apart and toes pointing forward. Relax the back and hang straight down. Alternate hanging toward the right leg, then the left.

Volume: Hold each stretch for 20 seconds.

Key points: Keep the knees straight and don't bounce.

FIRST BASEMAN STRETCH

Purpose: To improve flexibility of hips and quadriceps.

Procedure: Kneel with one leg in front of the other, forming a 90-degree angle. Place hands on top of the lead leg. Drive the hips forward while keeping the back arched and the chest out. Duplicate with opposing leg.

Volume: Hold each stretch for 20 seconds.

STANDING "X" STRETCH

Purpose: To improve flexibility of hamstrings.

Procedure: Stand with one leg crossed over the other. Relax the back and hang straight down. Switch legs and repeat.

Volume: Hold each stretch for 20 seconds.

Key points: Keep the knee of the back leg straight and don't bounce.

CATCHER'S STRETCH

Purpose: To improve flexibility of groin.

Procedure: Squat down as far as possible while keeping feet flat on the floor. Place elbows between knees and push knees outward. Try to squat deeper each time.

Volume: Hold each stretch for 20 seconds.

SHOULDER STRETCH 1

Purpose: To improve flexibility of rear deltoids and surrounding shoulder muscles.

Procedure: Stand with side up against wall. Extend arm behind body. Keep arm parallel to the ground and palm flat against the wall.

Volume: Hold stretch for 20 seconds.

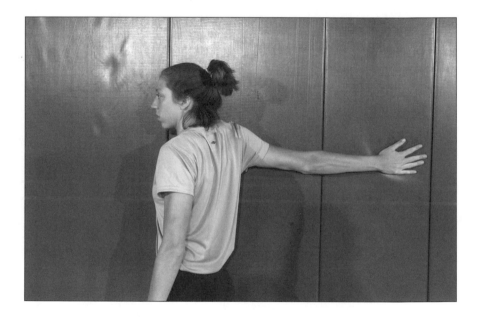

SHOULDER STRETCH 2

Purpose: To improve flexibility of rear deltoids and surrounding shoulder muscles.

Procedure: Stand facing the wall. Extend arm so that it's flat against the wall and parallel to the ground.

Volume: Hold stretch for 20 seconds.

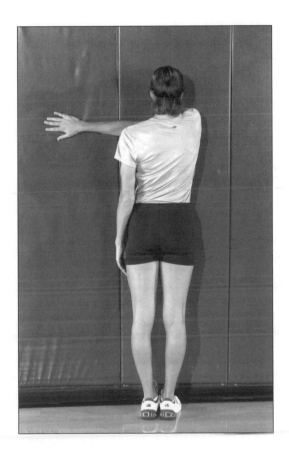

SHOULDER STRETCH 3

Purpose: To improve flexibility of rear deltoids and surrounding shoulder muscles.

Procedure: Stand with side up against the wall. Reach back behind the head. Keep elbow pointing upward and fingers pointing down.

Volume: Hold stretch for 20 seconds.

SPRINTER'S STRETCH

Purpose: To improve flexibility of calves.

Procedure: With both hands on the floor, extend one leg all the way back. Cross the opposite leg behind the extended leg. Keep the foot of the extended leg flat on the floor. Repeat with opposite leg.

Volume: Hold each stretch for 20 seconds.

DYNAMIC STRETCHES

SIDE LEG SWING

Purpose: To improve flexibility of torso, trunk, groin, and hips.

Procedure: Take hold of a solid structure with both hands and hold on in a comfortable position. Begin with shoulders, hips, and feet facing straight ahead. Swing the right leg out away from the body, then back across the body one time for each repetition. Duplicate with left leg.

Volume: Perform 10 reps with each leg.

Key points: Concentrate on taking small, controlled swings, gradually increasing the range of motion with each rep. Keep shoulders, hips, and feet facing straight ahead as the leg swings. Keep the trunk area tight and in control. Keep the knee of the swinging leg straight. Allow enough space for a full range of motion.

FORWARD LEG SWING

Purpose: To improve flexibility of torso, trunk, hips, and hamstrings.

Procedure: Find a solid structure to hold onto with both hands in a comfortable position. Start with shoulders, hips, and feet facing straight ahead. Swing the right leg out in front of the body, then back behind the body for each rep. Duplicate with left leg.

Volume: Perform 10 reps with each leg.

Key points: Take small, controlled swings, gradually increasing the range of motion with each rep. Keep shoulders, hips, and feet facing straight ahead as the leg swings. Keep trunk area tight and in control. Keep the knee of the swinging leg straight. Allow enough space to perform the exercise with a full range of motion.

SIDE LEG SWING (REPEAT)

Volume: Perform 10 reps with each leg.

Key points: During this second set, concentrate on taking bigger swings than during the first set.

FORWARD LEG SWING (REPEAT)

Volume: Perform 10 reps with each leg.

Key points: Concentrate on taking bigger swings than during the first set.

BAR DUCK

Purpose: To improve flexibility of torso, trunk, and hips.

Procedure: Find a raised object, such as a bar positioned in a squat rack. Place arms out in volleyball dig position. Keep feet, hips, and shoulders perpendicular to the bar. Place one foot beneath the bar and one foot on the other side of it. Begin the exercise by squatting beneath the bar. Finish by standing up on the other side of the bar. Repeat back and forth.

Volume: Perform 10 reps on each side.

Key points: Keep hands out in the dig position at all times. Keep hips lower than the shoulders at all times during the squat. Keep chest out and torso and head up at all times. Stay in control and be rhythmic.

Bar Duck

JOG WITH ARM SWING

Purpose: To warm up major joints and elevate body temperature.

Procedure: Jog at an easy pace. Swing arms in random patterns, back and forth across the body, front and back like a windmill. Be sure to move the arms continuously.

Volume: Jog the length of the court 2-4 times.

Key points: Keep it light. This is only the beginning of warm-up. Concentrate on breathing and focusing on the upcoming workout.

JOG WITH BUTT KICK

Purpose: To warm up nervous system and quadriceps.

Procedure: Jog straight ahead, quickly kicking heels up to the buttocks.

Volume: Jog the length of the court 2-4 times.

Key points: Keep knees pointing down. Concentrate on making fast foot strikes. The number of kicks performed within the length of the court is important, not how quickly you run.

JOG WITH HIGH KNEE

Purpose: To warm up nervous system, hamstrings, and hips.

Procedure: Jog straight ahead, quickly driving knees up to waist level.

Volume: Jog the length of the court 2-4 times.

Key points: Keep chest and shoulders driving forward, arms at 90-degree angles and swinging from the shoulders. Concentrate on fast foot strikes. As with butt kicks, the number of high-knee steps performed within the length of the court is most important.

DEEP SIDE SHUFFLE

Purpose: To improve flexibility of groin, hips, and hamstrings.

Procedure: Squat until the top of the thigh is parallel to the floor. Hold arms out in volleyball dig position. Shuffle slowly one step at a time, keeping the top of the thigh parallel with the floor.

Volume: Jog the length of the court 2-4 times.

Key points: Keep back arched, chest out, and shoulders back. Concentrate on staying low and feeling the stretch. Try to squat more deeply as you progress.

CARIOCA

Purpose: To improve flexibility of trunk.

Procedure: Hold arms out to side. Move laterally, crossing legs and arms over and back.

Volume: Jog the length of the court 2-4 times.

Key points: Keep the knee high as it crosses the body. Concentrate on opening and closing the hips.

REACH BACKS

Purpose: To improve flexibility of hamstrings.

Procedure: Jog backward, taking big strides.

Volume: Jog the length of the court 2-4 times.

Key points: Keep chest and shoulders leaning forward. Concentrate on taking big steps. Don't go too fast.

WALKING LUNGE

Purpose: To improve flexibility of hips, quadriceps, and hamstrings.

Procedure: Place hands on hips. Drive knee up to waist height and step forward. Repeat with opposite leg.

Volume: Jog the length of the court 2-4 times.

Key points: Keep back arched, chest out, and shoulders back. Concentrate on taking big, controlled steps. Don't let back knee touch the floor.

CHAPTER 3

CORE STABILITY AND POWER

For any athlete, the objective

of training is simple: to enhance performance and prevent injuries. Therefore, flexibility training and strength training go hand in hand.

For volleyball players, strength training begins by targeting what is known as the *power zone*. It is the center of the body that includes the abdomen, hips, and lower back. This chapter will deal primarily with abdominal exercises as the focus of training the power zone. While the lower back and hips also are strengthened by these exercises, greater attention will be devoted to those areas in chapter 7 (year-round conditioning). Building strength in these core areas will help develop strength and flexibility in sport-specific joints, such as the knees, ankles, and shoulders. When you develop a strong power zone and stable joints, everything else falls into place.

What makes the power zone so important? Here are a few reasons:

• Injury prevention. Many times, athletes will spend precious time off the court and in the training room because of abdominal strains and lower back pain. Volleyball involves repetitive motions such as swinging, jumping, and landing, which can adversely affect the abdomen and lower back throughout the season. The swing, for instance, taxes the abdominal muscles, and repeated landings take their toll on the lower back. In anticipation of this, it makes sense to prepare these areas for the intense demands that will be placed on them. Proper conditioning will significantly reduce injuries in all areas.

• Improved body control. The abdomen and lower back are the bridge connecting the upper body with the lower body. When the middle blocker is moving left to block a quick attack and then sees the setter deliver a combination X set to another attacker moving to the right, the upper half of the blocker's body must adjust and move to the right—no easy task, considering the momentum that forces the lower half of the body to continue moving left. If the bottom half of the body is moving

Holly McPeak has built strength in her power zone, which allows her to have great body control.

Steve Salmons

Steve Salmons was one of the great middle blockers who dominated the college game as a junior at UCLA. Salmons controlled the net for the Bruins' first undefeated team. When the U.S. team recruited him for a South American tournament, Salmons answered the call. Although he suffered a back injury during the summer tournament, he continued to play in every match. When he returned to UCLA, Salmons had developed severe scoliosis and could not straighten his back. Doctors recommended surgery, but Salmons decided instead to redshirt and rehabilitate his back through exercise.

Steve labored painstakingly to rehabilitate his spine while rigorously riding a stationary bicycle to retain leg strength and endurance. Almost two years after the Bruins' undefeated season, he returned to the court just one week before the conference playoffs. He played all five games of the NCAA finals, in which the Bruins defeated USC to win their eighth NCAA title. He was selected to the all-tournament team.

After leaving UCLA, Salmons played for the U.S. national team. Along with former UCLA teammate Karch Kiraly, he helped lead the United States to the triple crown of international volleyball—the Olympic gold medal in 1984, the World Cup Championship in 1985, and the World Championship in 1986.

Although it took 20 months of painful exercises, Salmons succeeded in strengthening his back and achieving the many accomplishments in the sport he loved.

in one direction and the upper half is moving in another, the athlete must call on something to get him or her back in sync as quickly as possible. That something is the strength of the power zone.

• Greater potential for body strength and power. Athletes must have a strong power zone to be able to train with heavier weights in the weight room and therefore become more powerful on the court. In the weight room, you're only going to be as strong as your lower back allows you to be. On the court, you're only going to be as powerful as your weight training has made you.

IMPORTANCE OF TRAINING ABS

The abdominal and lower back muscles are the bridge connecting the upper and lower body, so they encounter a great deal of stress. Therefore, any athlete must devote serious attention to maintaining those muscles. Volleyball players should integrate abdominal training into the beginning, middle, and end of their workouts. That conditions those muscles to perform almost constantly, as they do during a match or a game. A balance should be achieved between abdominal and lower back exercises.

Technique

Just because abdominal exercises ordinarily don't involve lifting any weight, that doesn't mean technique isn't important. On the contrary, it is *more* important because the risk of an injury to the lower back is at stake. Concentration on maintaining proper form is essential during abdominal work. Since isolating those muscles is difficult, an athlete must "feel" them being used.

When training abs, train them in a specific order. The abdominal muscles are divided into three parts: the obliques, the lower abs, and the upper abs. Obliques should be trained first, then the lower and upper abs. All three should be trained with equal intensity and duration.

Equipment

Everyone longs for perfectly conditioned abs. Many people spend an incredible amount of time in the gym using expensive machines that train only one area of the abdominal region. And late-night television is cluttered with infomercials espousing the benefits of one contraption or another guaranteed to produce rock-hard abs.

The truth is, you don't need a lot of fancy equipment to train your abdominal muscles properly. All you need is an 8-by-8-foot area, preferably matted; a set of metal plates ranging from 2.5 to 25 pounds; an adjustable flat bench; and a set of medicine balls ranging from 5 to 15 pounds. If you don't have medicine balls and can't afford them, try cutting open an old volleyball and filling it with sand. Experiment with using lighter filling material along with the sand to fill the ball to a desired weight, then tape it up tightly. The rest is up to you.

CRUNCHES

Purpose: To strengthen the abdominals.

Procedure: Lie on back on floor. Knees are bent with feet on the ground, and hands are behind the head. Slowly raise upper body toward knees using ab muscles.

Key points: Make sure the motion is slow and controlled.

CARDINAL ABS

Purpose: To strengthen the abdominals.

Procedure: Start lying down with knees slightly bent. Grab triceps behind your head. Raise upper torso off the ground to 45-degree angle and then lower back down

Key points: Make sure the movement is slow and controlled.

REGULAR ABDOMINALS

Purpose: To strengthen the upper abdominals.

Procedure: Lie on back with legs together and knees slightly bent. Keeping palms on the top of the legs and arms locked, raise torso until touching kneecaps. Return to starting position.

Key points: Keep arms fully extended and locked. Keep palms on top of legs, not off to the side. Stop at the kneecap.

Volume: Low to high intensity. No weight.

SIDE SIT-UP

Purpose: To strengthen the oblique abdominals.

Procedure: Lie on side with feet crossed for stability. Keep one hand behind head and lift upper torso off the floor.

Key points: Raise upper torso until the rib cage is not touching the floor. Be sure to stay on your side. Concentrate on keeping the oblique tight throughout the movement.

Volume: Low to high intensity. No weight.

KNEE UPS

Purpose: To strengthen the lower abdominals.

Procedure: Lie on back with legs extended and hands face down beneath the glutes. Bend knees to 90-degree angle. Kick legs back to starting position.

Key points: Keep lower back flat on the floor. Don't let feet touch the floor. Concentrate on keeping stomach tight.

Volume: Low to high intensity. No weight.

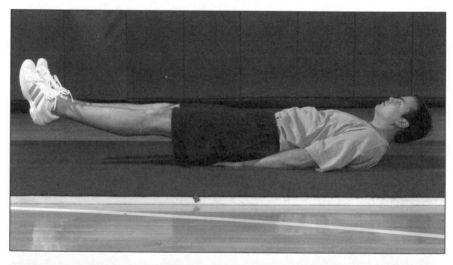

HIP UPS

Purpose: To strengthen the lower abdominals.

Procedure: Lie on back with legs extended out and hands face down under the glutes. Lift knees up to 90-degree angle by bending them. Once knees are up, kick legs straight up into extension, concentrating on hips coming up off the floor. Bring legs back to starting position.

Key points: Keep lower back flat on the floor. Keep feet from touching the floor. Concentrate on keeping the stomach tight throughout the movement.

Volume: Low to high intensity. No weight.

MEDICINE BALL SIT-UP THROW

Purpose: To strengthen the lower and upper abdominals.

Procedure: Lie on back with feet hooked with partner's for stability and knees bent at a 90-degree angle. Hold a medicine ball over the head with arms extended. Raise the upper torso off the floor, throwing the medicine ball to a partner at the same time.

Key points: Concentrate on throwing as hard as possible on the way up. Partner must throw the ball back high over the athlete's head to create a full stretch. Concentrate on keeping stomach tight throughout the movement.

Volume: High intensity with light weight. Low intensity with heavier weight.

MEDICINE BALL LONG THROW

Purpose: To strengthen the lower and upper abdominals.

Procedure: Lie on back with legs crossed and extended out and off the floor one to two inches. Hold a medicine ball over the head with arms extended. Raise the upper torso off the floor, throwing the medicine ball to a partner at the same time.

Key points: Concentrate on throwing on the way up as hard as possible. Don't let feet touch the floor. Keep upper torso off the floor while waiting for the ball. Partner must throw the ball back high over the athlete's head to achieve an optimum stretch.

Volume: High intensity with light weight. Low intensity with heavier weight.

TRAINING HIPS AND LOWER BACK

As important as the abdominal muscles, the hips and back should receive equal attention during a volleyball player's workout. These exercises should be incorporated into the routine with proper form being emphasized to avoid injury.

Strengthening the hips and lower back is essential because those muscles work in conjunction to prevent injuries and provide a solid strength foundation. Hip strength is important in any sport but particularly in those requiring the legs to extend to the side or across the body. Developing superior lateral movement is important for the success of any volleyball player, and strong hip muscles improve lateral strength, stability, and mobility.

SUPERMAN

Purpose: To strengthen the spinal erectors.

Procedure: Lie on stomach with arms extended over head. Keeping arms and legs extended straight, raise upper and lower torso off the floor at the same time. Hold for a count of two.

Key points: Concentrate on keeping the upper and lower torso rigid. Stay in control. Concentrate on keeping back tight throughout the movement. Perform with low to moderate intensity.

Volume: Low to high intensity. No weight.

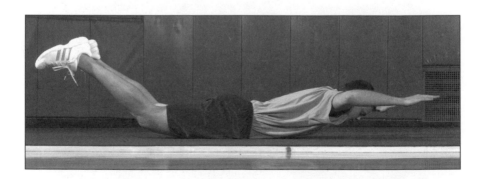

RUSSIAN TWIST

Purpose: To strengthen the obliques and lower back.

Procedure: Sit on the floor with feet in a stationary position. Keep arms extended straight out in a dig position. Lean upper torso back at a 45-degree angle. Turn upper torso from side to side, pausing briefly in the middle each time.

Key points: Keep hands up and arms extended throughout the exercise. Keep back arched and chest out. Concentrate on taking big, full turns. Keep stomach tight throughout the movement.

Volume: Low to high intensity. No weight.

WEIGHTED RUSSIAN TWIST

Purpose: To strengthen the obliques.

Procedure: With knees bent, hold a medicine ball extended in front of chest. Rotate the trunk.

Key points: Concentrate on full range of motion.

Volume: High intensity with light weight. Low intensity with heavier weight.

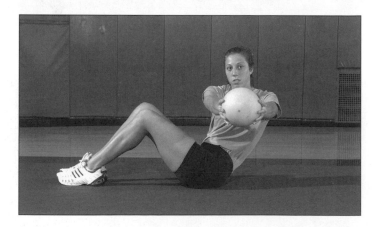

MEDICINE BALL SIDE THROWS

Purpose: To strengthen the obliques and lower back.

Procedure: Sit on the floor with legs apart. Hold a medicine ball with arms extended straight out in front. Rotate the upper torso and throw the ball to a partner off to the side. Repeat procedure for opposite side.

Key points: Keep hands and arms extended throughout the exercise. Concentrate on taking big, full turns. Concentrate on keeping the stomach tight throughout the movement.

Volume: High intensity with low weight. Low intensity with heavier weight.

REVERSE HYPEREXTENSION

Purpose: To strengthen the glutes and spinal erectors.

Procedure: Lie on stomach on raised bench with legs extended down so that the body is at a 90-degree angle. Keeping legs extended and knees locked, raise legs up until they are parallel to the floor. Hold for a count of two.

Key points: Concentrate on keeping legs locked straight throughout the range of movement.

Volume: Low to high intensity. No weight.

CHAPTER 4

STRENGTH
AND
EXPLOSIVENESS

Just about every volleyball coach

has used them and just about every volleyball player has performed them: *plyometrics,* or jump drills. What exactly are plyometrics? Where and when should they be done? How much is too much? These are all very important questions and ones that must be understood before setting up a quality jump program. This chapter will help to shed some light on this type of training and help you get started with a sound program.

Plyometrics are exercises that enable muscles to reach maximum strength in the shortest amount of time. Plyometrics use gravity to elicit what is called *stretch reflex* in muscles. Examples of this are box depth jumps and repeat verticals, both of which are familiar to volleyball players.

With both of these exercises, the body reacts to the ground. Both exercises have the athlete land on the ground and immediately take off back into the air. When the feet hit the ground, the body (specifically, the leg muscles) is forced to absorb the body's weight. This force is actually energy that can be used. The energy is stored in the muscles for a millisecond, then dissipates as the muscles relax. The key is to use this energy as quickly as possible to get back off the ground. That's what box depth jumps and repeat verticals are training the body to do.

Yet, it is not enough to know that plyometrics can be beneficial to jumping ability. You must understand how, why, when, and where to conduct these drills. This chapter will provide a simplified guideline for incorporating plyometrics into a regular workout.

Paula Weishoff

Paula Weishoff was a dominant middle blocker and server during a career that included two Olympic medals and induction into the Volleyball Hall of Fame in 1998. Durable and always superbly conditioned, Weishoff was able to extend her playing career into her late 30s, including nine seasons in the Italian League, despite the onset of knee problems that eventually required four surgeries.

"Today, knee injuries are very common among players," says Weishoff, an assistant coach at USC for the past five seasons. "A lot of volleyball players start at 12 and compete on weekends. It's an ongoing problem."

Weishoff played one season for USC before joining the U.S. national team in 1981. She won a silver medal in the 1984 games in Los Angeles and a bronze medal in 1992 in Barcelona. She also was a member of the 1996 team that competed in Atlanta. Weishoff went on to play in Italy, Brazil, and Japan, where she was named MVP after leading Daiei to the 1995 Japan pro league title.

To her credit, much of Weishoff's accomplishments came after her first knee surgery at age 27. She attributes her ability to rebound as well as her longevity to her years of dedication to intensive jump training.

"I did a lot of jumping rope and jump drills," Weishoff says. "Very gamelike [movements]. The biggest asset I had was my technique. We trained extremely hard, and I guess I always did a good job taking care of myself. We'd practice three times a week, and I'd be bored. I always did extra."

GUIDELINES

Before jumping into a routine of plyometrics, first develop a good strength base. As a general rule, athletes should be able to squat one-half times their body weight before performing plyometrics. To establish this, an athlete should first complete a 12-week program of leg work and lower back exercises to develop greater body awareness and awaken the nervous system. That means 12 weeks of closed chain exercises (squats, lunges, hang cleans, hang snatches, power cleans, power snatches, etc.) as well as the bevy of abdominal and lower back exercises devoted to strengthening the power zone, presented in chapter 7 (year-round conditioning). Progression should be gradual, with an emphasis on performing the exercise with proper technique and through a full range of motion.

Protect the jumper. There are several companies that provide soft materials to lay over hardwood basketball floors.

Joe Shirley

In 40 years of coaching at UCLA, I have had only one player take it upon himself to lead the key players through additional conditioning drills after practice was over. Joe Shirley was a backcourt substitute who made certain our starters were in better condition than our opponents. He would lead them on a run to Drake Stadium to jump up and down the grandstand steps or lead them up the stairwells in the tall buildings on campus.

Joe proved to be an important member of the Bruins' first NCAA championship team while setting a tradition for the program for years to come.

Location and Equipment

During the off-season, athletes should perform exercises on turf or grass to minimize stress. Performing exercises on a wooden court or concrete creates too much pounding on the joints and can result in problems such as shin splints, patellar tendentious (also known as jumper's knee), and back problems. Make sure the surface is level and free of moisture, potholes, or loose matter that could cause slips. When using boxes, make sure they are sturdy and well constructed. Many companies sell "stacking boxes" of various sizes (12 to 48 inches high), which will allow you to mix and match for each exercise. At any rate, make sure the boxes used have a nonslippery surface on top. Short carpet works well. Also, be sure the boxes do not have sharp edges. You'll know why the first time you miss your mark on a jump. If you don't have a lot of money or space, use bleachers, strong tables, or any raised surface that will hold up to the pressure. Just be careful and don't take any chances.

Proper attire also should be worn. That means good basketball or cross-training shoes that have thick soles and provide good support. Wear loose-fitting athletic clothing that allows freedom of movement. Taping ankles is a good idea, especially if you're prone to sprains. Otherwise, try to perform the drills without taping. In most cases, the drills will help develop tendon and ligament strength in the ankle.

Volleyball players favor light shoes but with thick soles that provide good support.

Proper Warm-Up

Before beginning, ride a stationary bicycle, jog, or perform some cardio-vascular exercise for 10 minutes to elevate the heart rate. Follow with 10 minutes of stretching exercises. Generally, plyometrics should be performed before weightlifting or conditioning drills. An exception can be made after progressing to movement-specific plyometrics. Then, the drills can be incorporated into conditioning and agility drills.

Progression

Jumps are divided into three categories: easy, moderate, and advanced. Easy jumps include tuck jumps, repeat verticals, jump and reach, and scissors jumps. Moderate jumps include standing box jumps, cord jumps, broad jumps, and lateral box jumps. Advanced jumps include depth jumps, single-leg jumps (vertical and lateral), and bounding. Movement-specific jumps can be added to any of the three categories. They are jumps that include blocker steps, arm swings, and arms held in a vertical block position.

Start out with basic drills and progress to movement-specific exercises after four to six weeks. Don't incorporate movement-specific drills until basic drills are mastered. Begin with low volume. Count the number of foot strikes to monitor volume. Begin with 40 to 50 strikes and work your way up to 160 to 200. Divide the foot strikes into sets and reps with an emphasis on performing quality strikes. Rest between sets. Remember, a tired athlete is a nonexplosive athlete.

EASY JUMPS

TUCK JUMP

Purpose: To improve vertical power.

Procedure: Stand on stable surface. Hold both arms straight out in front and parallel to the floor. Bend to 1/4 squat position, keeping chest up and back flat. Explode up by driving the knees up to the chest.

Volume: Start low and work up.

Key points: Concentrate on keeping the body in control. Overemphasize driving the knee up as high as possible. Try to limit the activity of the upper body during the jump. Swing the arms if necessary.

REPEAT VERTICAL

Purpose: To improve vertical power.

Procedure: Stand on stable surface. Hold both arms at side in 90-degree angle. Bend to 1/4 squat position, keeping chest up and back flat. Explode up off the floor. Land with legs bent so as to absorb the shock. Upon landing, accelerate back off the floor as quickly as possible.

Volume: Perform from 2 to 10 jumps at a time. Start low and work up in total volume.

Key points: Concentrate on keeping the body in control. Overemphasize quickness back up off the floor.

JUMP AND REACH

Purpose: To improve vertical power.

Procedure: Stand on stable surface. Hold both arms up with the palms facing outward in front of the shoulders. Bend to 1/4 squat position, keeping chest up and back tight. Explode up, extending above and in front of the head as if blocking.

Volume: Start low and work gradually to higher reps.

Key points: Concentrate on keeping the body in control. Overemphasize extending the body and reaching as high as possible with the arms.

SCISSORS JUMP

Purpose: To improve vertical power.

Procedure: Stand on stable surface with one foot in front of the other. Hold both arms at side at 90-degree angle. Squat down slightly, keeping chest up and back tight. Explode up by driving off equally with both feet. Once in the air, alternate legs in scissors action so that the opposite leg is now in front. Land with legs bent to absorb the shock. Upon landing, accelerate back off the floor as quickly as possible.

Volume: Perform anywhere from 2 to 10 jumps. Start low and increase volume to high reps.

Key points: Concentrate on keeping the body in control. Overemphasize quickness back off the floor.

MODERATE JUMPS

STANDING BOX JUMP

Purpose: To improve vertical power.

Procedure: Stand on a stable surface about two feet away from a stable raised surface. Hold both arms at the side at a 90-degree angle. Bend down to a 1/4 squat position, keeping chest up and back flat. Explode off the floor. Land with legs bent to absorb the shock.

Volume: Start low; increase to high reps.

Key points: Concentrate on keeping the body in control. Overemphasize total effort.

CORD JUMP

Purpose: To improve vertical power and endurance.

Procedure: Stand on stable surface. Hold both arms at side at 90-degree angle. Bend to 1/4 squat position, keeping chest up and back flat. Explode off the floor at a 45-degree angle. Land with legs bent to absorb the shock. Upon landing, accelerate back off the floor as quickly as possible 45 degrees in the opposite direction.

Volume: Start low and increase volume to high reps.

Key points: Concentrate on keeping the body in control. Overemphasize quickness back up off the floor.

BROAD JUMP

Purpose: To improve horizontal power.

Procedure: Stand on stable surface. Hold both arms at side at 90-degree angle. Bend to 1/4 squat position, keeping chest up and back flat. Explode directly out in front. Land with legs bent to absorb the shock. Upon landing, accelerate back off the floor as quickly as possible.

Volume: Perform 2 to 10 jumps. Start low; increase volume with higher reps.

Key points: Concentrate on keeping the body in control. Overemphasize quickness back up off the floor.

LATERAL BOX JUMP

Purpose: To improve lateral power.

Procedure: Stand on stable surface. Hold both arms at side at 90-degree angle. Bend to 1/4 squat position, keeping chest up and back flat. Explode off the floor onto a raised platform positioned directly to the side. Land with legs bent to absorb the shock.

Volume: Start low; increase volume with higher reps.

Key points: Concentrate on keeping the body in control. Overemphasize not turning into the jump. Keep hips and shoulders square.

ADVANCED JUMPS

DEPTH JUMP

Purpose: To improve vertical power.

Procedure: Stand on stable raised surface. Hold both arms at side at 90-degree angle. Step off the raised surface down to the floor. Land with legs bent to absorb the shock. Upon landing, accelerate back off the ground as quickly as possible and land on the higher surface positioned directly in front.

Volume: Start low; increase volume with higher reps.

Key points: Concentrate on keeping the body in control. Overemphasize quickness back up off the ground.

SINGLE LEG JUMP

Purpose: To improve vertical power.

Procedure: Various plyometric exercises can be performed with one leg.

Volume: Start low; increase volume with higher reps.

Key points: Concentrate on keeping the body in control. Overemphasize safe leg mechanics. Only advanced athletes should perform these jumps. Drill should be performed only after mastery of other plyometric exercises is attained and adequate strength level is apparent.

STRAIGHT-AHEAD BOUND

Purpose: To improve vertical and horizontal power.

Procedure: Stand on cushioned surface with one foot in front of the other. Hold both arms at side at 90-degree angle. Squat slightly, keeping chest up and back tight. Explode forward by driving off the front foot. Once in the air, alternate legs in scissors action so the opposite leg is now in front. Land with legs bent to absorb the shock. Upon landing, accelerate back off the ground as quickly as possible.

Volume: Perform 10 to 20 jumps. Start low; increase volume with higher reps.

Key points: Concentrate on keeping the body in control. Overemphasize quickness back off the ground.

LATERAL BOUND

Purpose: To improve vertical power while on the move.

Procedure: Start in volleyball ready position. Bound up off the floor sideways by driving off with trail leg. Continue and increase distance.

Volume: Perform at varying distances.

Key points: Concentrate on keeping the body in control. Overemphasize height and distance with each jump.

LATERAL CONE HOPS

Purpose: To improve lateral quickness.

Procedure: Jump over the cone from side to side.

Key points: Concentrate on getting off the ground quickly.

CHAPTER 5

HONING AGILITY AND QUICKNESS

Volleyball is a sport of various movement patterns. Rallies typically last anywhere between 8 and 15 seconds, but some can last as long as a half-minute, requiring players to jump, dive, and often sprawl all over the court. To be sure, the game is played much more rapidly than it was in the 1960s, when blocking over the net was prohibited and players seldom dove to the floor unless they tripped. The vertical and lateral aspects of the game are more important today than ever before.

Agility drills can help the middle back defender run to a ball deflected by the middle blocker. Some of the larger arenas have between 30 and 40 feet of playing surface behind the end line, and an agile defender is able to run down balls and keep them in play.

The quick offenses used today require players to be exceptionally agile and athletic on both sides of the net. In 2002, UCLA lost to UC Santa Barbara in the opening round of the playoffs because Bruin blockers were not agile and quick enough to get to the point of attack before the spiker hit the ball. Since the spiker's arm is moving faster than the blocker's arm, the blocker must be there first to succeed. For example, when our right-side blocker is bunched 10 feet from the sideline to help defend against a quick set to the opponent's middle attacker, he must also be able to move quickly to the antenna to defend against a slightly higher set to the outside attacker. When the opponent passes our serve accurately, our right-side blocker must also defend against the opponent's right-side attacker crossing behind the middle attacker or a player hitting a short set out of the middle back. Any hesitation by the blocker on a perfect pass usually results in success by the opponent.

Therefore, movement drills have become an important aspect to volleyball conditioning. Most effective are those modeled after movement patterns that take place on the court.

The blockers did not touch this ball because they have to be over the net before the spiker hits the set.

Danny Farmer

A few years ago, UCLA's Danny Farmer was playing defense in the left back in an NCAA semifinal match against Lewis University in the Stan Sheriff Center in Hawaii. The underdog Lewis team led 13-12 in the fourth game when Danny took off after a deflected spike. Although the middle back defender had a 10-foot head start on Danny, he got to the ball first, reached into the stands, and hit the ball back to the frontcourt with a right-hand roundhouse dig. The Bruins went on to win the rally and the game, 15-13. Danny was not only a middle blocker for the volleyball team but also a starting wide receiver for the UCLA football team (and is now a member of the Cincinnati Bengals). Agility drills helped immensely in his development as an athlete in both sports.

CHANGES IN VOLLEYBALL

Today's volleyball players are once again allowed to receive serves with their hands, as was the rule 40 years ago. The difference today is that there is a much more liberal interpretation of how long a player may hold onto the ball. In the old days, infractions for overhand contact were called more strictly. Double hits on the serve reception and the first contact of the serve and spiked ball are allowed. The serve and first contact of the spiked ball can be double-hit in college, club, and all international matches. The result is longer rallies and fewer whistles.

Agility exercises should be performed with an emphasis on gradual progression. Before beginning a program, athletes should complete four to six weeks of basic aerobic exercises and conditioning drills. This helps prevent injury when more demanding movements are placed on the body.

Athletes should begin with distance sprints of 400 and 800 meters to develop a strong aerobic base before beginning a set of agility exercises. They should be performed with a 1:1 ratio, meaning that an athlete should rest for a period equal in length to the time it took to run a designated distance. The sprint should be started from a jog and end

Beach volleyball requires more endurance than the indoor game.

with a jog to prevent muscle injury. During the first four weeks, basic movement drills with no change in direction (side shuffle, backpedaling, and walking lunge) should be incorporated, but they should be performed on a track or grass field. The following 8 to 12 weeks are designed to include aerobic and anaerobic workouts and a progression to change-of-direction drills (widths, four corners, short shuttle, V drill, box drill, and T-drills).

BASIC MOVEMENT DRILLS

SIDE SHUFFLE

Purpose: To improve lateral movement.

Procedure: Start in volleyball ready position. Shuffle sideways, staying low with knees bent, chest out, and back tight.

Volume: Perform at varying distances.

Key points: Concentrate on keeping the body under control. Overemphasize staying low.

BACKPEDALING

Purpose: To improve foot speed.

Procedure: Start in volleyball ready position. Run backward, staying low with knees bent, chest out, and back tight.

Volume: Perform at varying distances.

Key points: Concentrate on keeping the body under control. Overemphasize staying low.

WALKING LUNGE

Purpose: To improve agility and balance.

Procedure: Start with hands on hips, chest out, and back tight. Step out as far as possible with one leg. Bend down, rise up, and then do the same with the other leg.

Volume: Perform at varying distances.

Key points: Concentrate on keeping the body in control. Overemphasize big steps with the knee never driving over the toes.

CHANGE-OF-DIRECTION DRILLS

WIDTHS

Purpose: To improve foot speed and change of direction.

Procedure: Starting on one sideline, sprint to opposite sideline. On arriving at the sideline, turn by lowering hips, bending knees, and planting one foot, and sprint back. Repeat back and forth as many times as time permits.

Volume: Perform six sets, 12 seconds each.

Key points: Concentrate on keeping body in control. Overemphasize being athletic on the turn.

FOUR CORNERS

Purpose: To improve reactive agility.

Procedure: Starting in the center of one side of the court, stand in volleyball ready position. The coach points to a corner, and you react by sprinting over and touching that corner with a hand. Then sprint back to center position ready for the next command. The coach changes the corner, and you repeat the drill. Repeat as many times as time permits.

Volume: Perform six sets of 12 seconds.

Key points: Concentrate on keeping body in control. Overemphasize being athletic on the turn.

SHORT SHUTTLE

Purpose: To improve foot speed.

Procedure: Starting in the center of one side of the court, stand in volleyball ready position. Turn and sprint to the sideline. On arriving at sideline, turn by lowering hips, bending knees, and planting one foot, and sprint back to opposite sideline. Sprint back to center position to finish the drill.

Volume: Perform multiple sets.

Key points: Concentrate on keeping the body under control. Overemphasize being athletic on the turn.

V DRILL

Purpose: To improve foot speed and change of direction.

Procedure: Set up three cones 15 feet apart in the form of a wide "V." Start at one cone and sprint to the second cone. On reaching the second cone, bring the body under control and side shuffle to the third and final cone.

Volume: Perform multiple sets in both directions.

Key points: Concentrate on keeping the body under control. Overemphasize cutting the corner sharply, not rounding it.

BOX DRILL

Purpose: To improve lateral movement and change of direction.

Procedure: Set up four cones 15 feet apart in the shape of a box. Start at one cone and sprint to the second cone. On reaching the second cone, bring the body under control and side shuffle to the third cone. On reaching the third cone, bring the body under control and backpedal to the fourth cone. On reaching the fourth cone, bring the body under control and side shuffle back to the cone that was the starting point.

Volume: Perform multiple sets in both directions.

Key points: Face the same direction throughout the drill. Concentrate on keeping the body under control. Overemphasize cutting the corners sharply, not rounding them.

T DRILL

Purpose: To improve lateral movement.

Procedure: Set up four cones 15 feet apart in the form of a "T." Start at the bottom of the T and sprint ahead to the next cone. On reaching the second cone, bring the body under control and side shuffle to the third cone. On reaching the third cone, bring the body under control and side shuffle to the fourth cone. On reaching the fourth cone, bring the body under control and side shuffle back to the second cone. Bring the body under control and backpedal to the first cone.

Volume: Perform multiple sets.

Key points: Face the same direction throughout the drill. Concentrate on keeping the body under control. Overemphasize sharp corners, not rounding them.

CHAPTER 6

COURT DRILLS

A key to winning volleyball

is conducting practice sessions that incorporate a wide variety of conditioning and game condition drills that change frequently enough to interest and motivate players. The drills that have been selected here allow the athletes to condition the muscles needed to excel in volleyball. The drills have been used on the UCLA practice floor for many years.

The first 17 drills do not require diagrams and are rather simple warmup and conditioning exercises. As volleyball techniques receive more emphasis, the drills become more complex and are diagrammed and identified by one of the following techniques: conditioning, serving and passing, setting, spiking, blocking, and digging.

Mike Normand

The man who introduced the conditioning exercise known as the circle drill was a former UCLA player and assistant coach, "Storming" Mike Normand, whose legacy is well entrenched in Westwood. Ten years after Normand introduced the drill he continued to lead players around the gym, exhorting them to perform push-ups and sit-ups as quickly and as well as he did. This created a great deal of competition between the players and Coach Normand. Since Normand stood 5 feet, 10 inches, many players towered over him and outweighed him by as much as 40 pounds.

Coach Normand supervised the UCLA volleyball weight training in 1987 and devised a grading scale of weight training based on Olympic lifts by body weight. As it turned out, Normand was the champion and players became very determined to beat him. So much, in fact, that the 1987 UCLA team became one of the program's best conditioned teams ever and went 38-3 en route to an NCAA championship.

For freshman Mark Tedsen, the season contained an added highlight. Tedsen became the first player to defeat Normand in weightlifting and immediately became one of the most popular players on the team.

CONDITIONING DRILLS

CONE DRILL

Purpose: To develop change of direction and build anaerobic strength in a timed drill.

Procedure: Place one cone in the center of the court and eight cones around it in a circle with a diameter of 30 feet. A player starts at one of the outside cones, runs to touch the middle cone, then runs back to touch the next outside cone, back to touch the middle cone, and so on.

Key points: Focus on changing direction as quickly and efficiently as possible. Two players can begin in opposite directions at the same time. The first person back to the origin is the winner.

Equipment and personnel: Nine cones; 2 to 12 players.

ELASTIC JUMP

Purpose: To incorporate plyometric exercises into a quick and easy warm-up.

Procedure: Tie a long elastic band to one of the poles and weave it through a line of approximately eight players standing along the net. The rest of the team jumps through the line, then waits at the end and returns after all the jumpers have reached the other side.

Key points: Space players so that the jumping players can land and jump again immediately without having to reshuffle their feet.

Equipment and personnel: One 15-foot elastic band for every 12 players.

SETTING SIT-UPS

Purpose: To develop abdominal strength and setting skills.

Procedure: A player lies on his or her back, knees slightly bent and apart. This player is the setter. The tosser stands 10 feet from the setter and tosses the ball while the setter executes a sit-up and sets the ball back to the tosser. Continue for 30 to 60 seconds, switch positions, and continue.

Key points: The setter extends the arm and follows through to set a high ball back to the tosser. To increase difficulty, the setter should set balls farther away. A weighted volleyball can be used to help shoulder and hand strength, and the tosser can use two balls to speed up the drill.

Equipment and personnel: One ball for every 2 players; 2 to 24 players on one court.

SIT-UP CIRCLE

Purpose: To develop abdominal/oblique strength while working with teammates.

Procedure: The team forms a circle with each player approximately one arm's distance apart. Then the players sit down with every other player's feet facing inward, flat on the floor, knees at approximately 90 degrees and leaning back approximately 45 degrees. The other players lie on their backs with their feet facing the seated players. As the seated player rotates the torso to take a ball from the player who is executing a sit-up, that player then rotates and hands off to the player on the other side. One player is doing sit-ups and the other player is doing torso rotations. Two, three, or four balls can be used. Continue the drill for 45 to 60 seconds. Rest for 30 to 45 seconds and then rotate positions.

Key points: Players doing sit-ups should be spaced far enough apart so that they must reach for the ball. Seated players should be leaning back to work the obliques during torso rotation. To make the drill more interesting, time how long it takes for the ball to travel around the entire circle, or execute the drill until the ball travels around the circle a designated number of times. Switch the direction of the ball during the exercise and use weighted balls for added resistance.

Equipment and personnel: Two to four medicine balls; 6 to 18 players.

AROUND THE WORLD SIT-UPS

Purpose: To develop abdominal and lower-body core strength.

Procedure: The team forms a circle, with approximately three feet between each player. Players lie on their backs along the line with knees bent at approximately 90 degrees. Each player has a ball and sends it clockwise around the circle while performing sit-ups. Perform 20 sit-ups, rest for 45 to 60 seconds, and repeat.

Key point: Space the team to perform the type of sit-up that you require (crunch or full range).

Equipment and personnel: One ball for each player; six or more players.

TOUCH, REACT, SLIDE

Purpose: To develop lower body core strength and reactionary lateral quickness.

Procedure: Player A stands on a line facing a tosser, who is eight feet away and holding a ball. Two other players stand to the left and right of player A on the same line. The drill begins when player A runs to touch the ball and then backs up to the line. As soon as player A reaches the line, the tosser sends the ball to one of the side players, who sends it back to the tosser. Player A quickly reacts and slides to touch the knee of the player who caught the ball and then slides back to the center to continue the drill. After each return to the center, player A goes forward to touch the ball in the tosser's hand. Continue the drill for 20 to 35 seconds. Rotate players and continue until each player performs a minimum of three sets.

Key points: Player A should be balanced in a flexed knee position when returning to the line after the first touch, with feet shoulder-width apart. Slide players can be moved away from player A. Player A can then use a three-step crossover move to reach the side players. To place a much greater workload on the muscles, player A can touch the shoe of the tosser and side players.

Equipment and personnel: One ball for every four players.

LATERAL JUMPING

Purpose: To develop lower-body core strength while working on blocking technique.

Procedure: A player starts in a flexed knee position, with feet shoulder-width apart. Without a step, the player bounds to the left and, without stepping or reshuffling feet, bounds back to the right. Continue for 12 to 15 repetitions and rest for 30 to 40 seconds.

Key points: The player's feet should hit the floor simultaneously, approximately shoulder-width apart. The player should land balanced, gather, and bound back to the other side. Add a slide step and crossover steps at the net to hone footwork technique.

Equipment and personnel: One or more players at the net.

LATERAL MOVEMENT

Purpose: To develop lower-body core strength through lateral movement.

Procedure: Two players stand on a line 15 feet apart. A third player starts at one side and, as quickly as possible, moves from one player to the other. At each end, the third player must touch the standing player's knee. Continue for 15 to 20 seconds, rotate players, and complete three to five sets.

Key points: The player should be in a low position without crossing the feet for the first few sets and should use the crossover step for the remainder of the sets. Shorten length to work on a quicker, more explosive change of direction. The third player can touch the shoe of the standing player to add a partial squat. This drill can be a race between teammates.

Equipment and personnel: Three or more players.

THREE-MAN WEAVE

Purpose: To develop change of direction and quick short sprints using an anaerobic drill.

Procedure: Three players line up in the middle of the court on the end line. The tosser has a cart of balls and is positioned at the middle of the net. The tosser throws the first player a ball high and toward the far corner. That player must run and set the ball high, back to one of the two target players stationed by the net antenna. As soon as the tosser throws the ball and the first player releases, another ball is tossed in the opposite direction for the next player in line. The third player runs for a toss, and then, without breaking the rhythm, the players weave back and forth on the end line.

Key points: The tosser should vary tosses slightly to keep players spaced. Depending on the speed of the players, tosses can go farther or lower to increase the demand on the athletes. The drill can be performed for a designated time or a designated number of perfect sets.

Equipment and personnel: Six balls, one ball cart, and 5 to 12 players.

DEFENSIVE MIRROR

Purpose: To incorporate defensive floor techniques into overall conditioning and warm-up.

Procedure: Choose a large area of the court. One player is the leader, facing the rest of the players who are spread out on the court. When the whistle blows, the entire team begins running in place. The leader then executes a volleyball skill that the team mirrors. The move should take the players to the floor and then back to their feet as quickly as possible. Each time the players return to their feet, the leader uses a block jump or spike approach before returning to the floor. Rest for 30 to 45 seconds and then repeat.

Key points: Players should have enough space between them to avoid collisions. The leader should wait long enough for most of the team to return to their feet to keep the slowest members in the drill. Use rolls, dives, and sprawls to the front, back, left, and right.

Equipment and personnel: Up to six players on each half of the court.

ELASTIC CORD BLOCKING

Purpose: To develop sound technical blocking skills and lower-core strength.

Procedure: Stretch a thin, elastic cord between the antennas, approximately eight inches above the height of the net. Blockers execute blocking moves and penetrate over the net and under the elastic cord. Perform 10 to 15 blocking moves per set. Rest one to two minutes between sets.

Key points: Blockers stay balanced in their movements. To develop core strength, blockers should use explosive movements. The blockers can execute moves along the length of the net or work in another area. They can travel along the net using a slide step, using a two- to three-step crossover, or by turning and running.

Equipment and personnel: Volleyball court, antennas, elastic cord, and 3 to 12 players.

BLOCKING MOVES

Purpose: To develop lower-body core strength through sound, balanced blocking techniques.

Procedure: Two players stand on chairs 10 feet apart, holding balls firmly over the top of the net. The blockers face them on the other side of the net and start in good blocking position. The blockers move back and forth between the balls, blocking each one and traveling by executing a crossover step and jump. Do 12 to 20 repetitions.

Key points: The blocker should have arms extended before the jump. Place the chairs 15 feet apart and execute a long first step and crossover step. Hold the balls farther off the net to work on hand penetration.

Equipment and personnel: Two chairs, two volleyballs, and 3 to 12 players.

APPROACH AND BLOCK TRANSITION

Purpose: To develop lower-body strength and conditioning while incorporating transition footwork training.

Procedure: Two players line up across the net from one another. Without a ball, one player begins as the attacker 15 to 20 feet off the net. The other player is the blocker starting at the net. As the hitter approaches, the blocker adjusts to the hitter's approach and executes a maximum block while the hitter simulates a spike after the approach. The blocker then uses transition footwork to get enough depth for a three-step approach while the partner blocks. The players keep the transition going for the length of the drill. Continue for 25 to 30 seconds.

Key points: The blocker should adjust to the hitter's approach and have legs loaded to jump before executing the block. The hitter should vary approach angles and simulate different types of shots (i.e., line, angle tip, and roll). Transition off the net should be a three- or four-step crossover (as opposed to backpedaling).

Equipment and personnel: Volleyball court and 2 to 12 players.

UP AND BACK

Purpose: To develop lower-body strength through forward and backward movement while maintaining good ball control.

Procedure: The passer starts on the three-meter line. The tosser should be on the opposite three-meter line with a cart of balls. At the net is a player acting as a target. The first ball is tossed short to the passer and, after passing it, the passer immediately backs up to approximately the 25-foot area to receive the next ball from the tosser. Continue for 25 to 30 seconds. Rotate from tosser to passer to target.

Key points: Toss balls to make the passer work hard but in the range for controlled execution. Low balls should be played with the forearms and high balls taken with the hands. The ball can be tossed from a crosscourt or straight-ahead position. The target location should be where you want your team to pass the serve. This drill can continue for a designated time or a specified number of perfect passes.

Equipment and personnel: A cart of balls and 3 to 12 players.

TIP DRILL

Purpose: To develop lower-body core strength and balance while in a low defensive position.

Procedure: One player assumes a low defensive position while a teammate tips a ball from above the head at the first player. The defensive player remains low throughout the drill and digs the tip high and back to the teammate. Continue the drill for 20 to 30 seconds. Players rest while switching positions.

Key points: The defensive player should maintain a knee angle as close to 90 degrees as possible throughout the set. The tipped ball should be dug 15 to 20 feet high. The player tipping the ball can jump and tip or tip over the net, in which case a third target player needs to be added on the defensive player's side of the net.

Equipment and personnel: Six balls and 2 to 12 players.

DIG, SPRAWL, RUN

Purpose: To develop upper- and lower-body strength during the execution of defensive techniques.

Procedure: The coach stands on a platform with a cart of balls. A group of three players is on the sideline across the net. The first player receives three balls in succession from the coach: a spiked ball, a tip, and a toss to run down. Do five to eight repetitions per group.

Key points: Hit the first ball about 20 feet down the line. As soon as the ball is dug, tip the next ball five feet from the net, forcing the player to go onto the floor to dig the ball. Then toss the third ball high toward the corner so that the player must quickly get up and sprint to play the ball back high and to the center of the court. Each player starts in the assigned defensive position. The next player in line begins as soon as the preceding player contacts the third ball.

Equipment and personnel: A cart of balls, a platform to stand on, and 4 to 12 players.

REACT AND ATTACK

Purpose: To develop reactionary quickness while training attacking skills.

Procedure: The coach stands at the middle of the net, back to the net. A player stands 20 to 25 feet off the net. As the player begins to approach the coach, the coach turns and faces the right or left side of the court and tosses a set that the approaching player attacks. The player's first move should be directly at the coach before making the adjustment to attack the ball. The player must begin far enough off the net to get a good approach.

Key points: As the player improves, toss the ball lower to speed up reaction time. Add a setter to set front or back as soon as the hitter can hit the lower toss.

Equipment and personnel: A cart of balls and 1 to 12 players.

DRILLS WITH DIAGRAMS

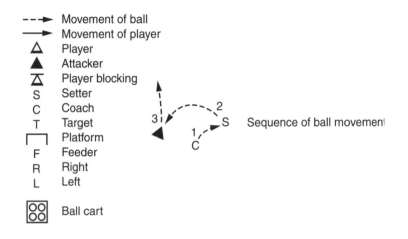

--→ Movement of ball
——→ Movement of player
△ Player
▲ Attacker
◬ Player blocking
S Setter
C Coach
T Target
⌐⌐ Platform
F Feeder
R Right
L Left

⊞ Ball cart

Sequence of ball movement

Key to diagrams.

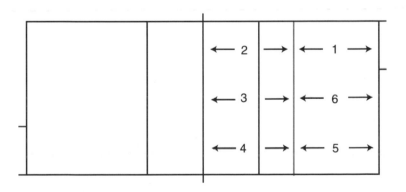

Serving specific areas.

SPIKE, RECOVER, SPIKE

Purpose: To increase endurance while improving spiking skills.

Procedure: The coach throws the ball to the setter, and the spiker tries to put the ball away against a two-person block. The extra players shag balls and return them to the feeder. After 10 spikes, the first spiker rests while another player spikes 10 balls. The resting spiker makes sure that the blocked balls are cleared from under the active spiker's feet. The drill is repeated two to three times, depending on the condition of the spikers.

Key points: This type of interval training is time consuming, particularly with large groups. If a team does not have adequate gym time, interval training can be done off the court using a series of 70-yard sprints from a jogging start and stop.

Equipment and personnel: Ten balls, a ball cart, one coach, and 8 to 12 players.

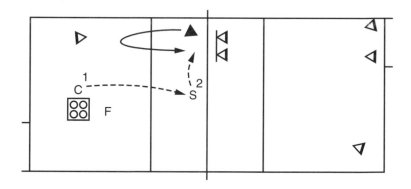

SPIKE AND DIVE

Purpose: To increase endurance while working on the quick hit and dive.

Procedure: The coach at the net tosses a quick set for the spiker. As the spiker returns to the floor, the coach in back tosses a ball for the spiker to dive for. The player then gets up and goes to the end of the line; meanwhile the player acting as the target returns the ball to the feeder in the backcourt. The shaggers on the other side of the net return the ball to the spiking line feeder. Ten spikes and 10 dives with five to six players moving through the drill in a rapid manner comprise one set. Each player can go through the drill one, two, or three times, depending on the intensity of the training session and technical and physical ability.

Key points: The spiker should dig the ball high in the air in the center of the court.

Equipment and personnel: Ten balls, a ball cart, two coaches, and 10 to 12 players.

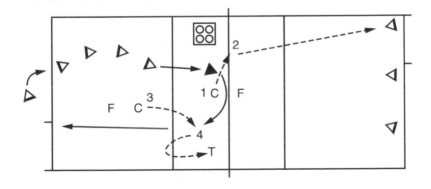

REPETITIVE SPIKES

Purpose: To increase two players' endurance while working on another player's passing technique.

Procedure: The coach serves to the player in area 5, and the setter backsets the area 5 player's pass to the area 2 spiker while the area 4 player on the coach's side blocks. After blocking, the area 4 player receives a set from the coach and the area 2 player blocks. If the ball is not dug by the area 5 player, the coach serves another ball to area 5 and the drill is repeated. If the area 5 player does dig the ball, the setter delivers a backset and the drill is repeated. The area 4 spiker should be replaced after 10 spikes and blocks but can come back after the next player is done.

Key point: The starting player who is the poorest passer should pass from the weakest passing position.

Equipment and personnel: Ten balls, a ball cart, one coach, and 8 to 12 players.

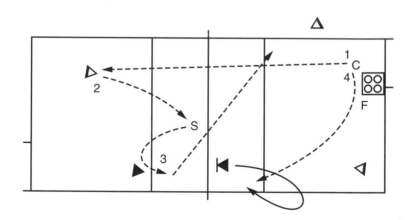

REPETITIVE DEEP SPIKES

Purpose: To increase endurance and improve the ability to spike deep sets.

Procedure: The coach stands in area 3 and alternately lobs sets to areas 4 and 2 about 10 feet from the net. The spikers try to put the ball away against the diggers in areas 5, 6, and 1. Another player stands in front of the net to serve as a target for the diggers and to prevent a ball from going under the spiker's feet. The target player puts balls in the cart for the coach. Players not involved in the drill serve as shaggers.

Key points: The coach should lob the sets far enough from the net so that the backcourt players have a chance to dig the ball. This distance will vary according to the ability of the spikers.

Equipment and personnel: Ten balls, a ball cart, a coach, and 8 to 12 players.

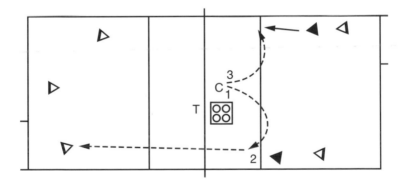

QUICK HITTER BLOCK AND SPIKE REPETITIVELY

Purpose: To increase endurance and to transition quickly from blocking to attacking.

Procedure: The coach stands on a platform and spikes balls off the blockers' hands to the backcourt. The middle blocker drops off the net as the ball is dug to the setter and approaches and spikes a quick set. Two blockers oppose the quick hitter, and if they block the ball back into the spiker's court, the teammates pass the block rebound to the setter and the quick hitter spikes again. If the defense digs the ball, the defending team tries to score using its quick hitter. When the ball is dead, the coach hits another ball at the blockers.

Key points: Quick hitters use a one-, two-, or three-step approach on the transition from blocking to spiking, depending on the amount of time they have. The point is that they jump as the setter is contacting the ball.

Equipment and personnel: Ten balls, a ball cart, a platform, a coach, and 12 players.

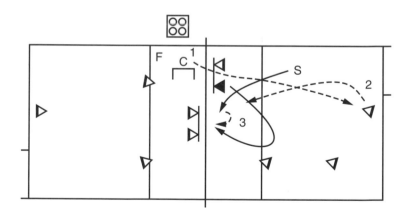

AREA 2 VERSUS AREA 4 SPIKER

Purpose: To increase players' endurance while working on spiking and blocking skills in a highly competitive drill.

Procedure: The coach throws the ball to the setter, and the spiker in area 4 tries to put the ball away against a full defense. If the defense digs the ball, it is set to the area 2 spiker, and the player in area 4 blocks. Play continues until the ball hits the floor. The coach on the side of the net that lost the rally tosses the ball into play to initiate the next rally. A point is scored on each rally, and the team that gets to 10 points first wins. Players rotate until everyone who spikes and blocks in areas 2 and 4 participates in those positions.

Key points: Because this is an endurance drill, the coach must put the ball into play as soon as the ball is dead so that there is no time to rest. To ensure intense competition, match up first-team players opposite each other in areas 2 and 4.

Equipment and personnel: As many balls as are available divided into two ball carts; two coaches and 12 players.

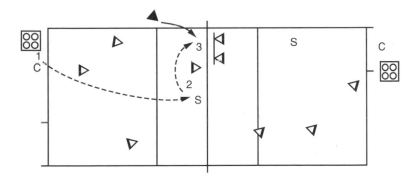

SERVING AND PASSING DRILLS

FOREARM PASS WITH SLIDE STEP

Purpose: To teach the passer to move laterally using a slide step to get into position behind the ball.

Procedure: Two tossers, each with a ball, stand with their backs to the net and alternately two-hand underhand toss their balls to the passer. The passer moves from side to side, stepping laterally, stepping first with the outside foot and then quickly sliding the trailing foot toward the lead foot. This action is repeated until the passer lines up with the oncoming ball, whereupon the feet stop and the passer directs the ball back to the first tosser. The second tosser lets the second ball go, and the passer slides back again to line up with the oncoming ball. The action is repeated until the ball is contacted a specified number of times by the passer, whereupon the passer becomes a tosser.

Key points: The passer should be coached to stop the feet before the ball is contacted, even if not yet behind the ball. This will enable the passer to better control the forearm placement. This drill is for all levels, from elementary school to college.

Equipment and personnel: Three players; two balls.

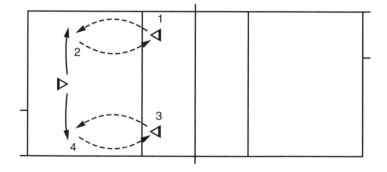

FOREARM PASS WITH SHUFFLE STEP

Purpose: To teach the passer to move laterally and forward without crossing the legs. This enables the passer better body control and should result in a better pass.

Procedure: Two tossers stand with their backs to the net and alternately toss balls to the passer. The passer is in a serve receiving position and quickly moves toward the tossed ball, stepping with the outside foot first. The passer quickly returns to the starting position after the pass and then reacts to the next tossed ball. Time the drill, having each of the three players pass for four minutes.

Key points: A wall and a line can be used to simulate a net and a sideline if there are not enough courts. Make sure that the passer moves quickly and stops with the feet farther than shoulder-width apart to provide a wide base of support for better balance. Use this drill at the beginning of every season. Proper footwork is important.

Equipment and personnel: Three players; two balls.

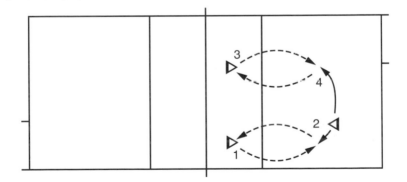

ACE THE PASSER

Purpose: To train an advanced passer to cover more territory when receiving serves and to teach the servers to keep the ball away from the passer.

Procedure: One primary passer covers the entire court. The servers attempt to ace the passer by hitting deep corners or short frontcourt areas.

Key points: Use this drill before playing an opponent with a libero who takes most of the serves. The first team should serve against your best passer.

Equipment and personnel: One ball for each server; 4 to 12 players.

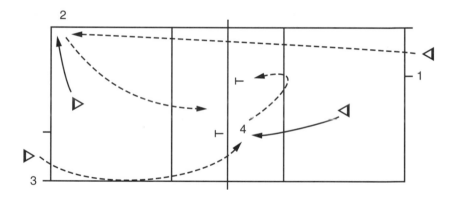

SETTING DRILLS

SETTING FROM AREA 6

Purpose: To train the middle back player to set high to the corners of the net.

Procedure: Two target players are placed in the front corners of the court by the net and two feeders are placed near the end line and sideline. Four players form a line in area 6 by the end line and react to the balls the feeders deliver to them. Each player calls "Mine!" and delivers a high set to one of the target players, then returns to the end of the line as the target player quickly sets a low ball back to the feeder for continuous action. The feeders control the intensity of the drill by first giving the players balls they can set overhand and then increasing the players' range, causing them to bump-set and finally dive and roll to bump-set the ball.

Key point: Players should get to the ball as quickly as possible and set from a stationary position whenever possible.

Equipment and personnel: Two balls; eight players.

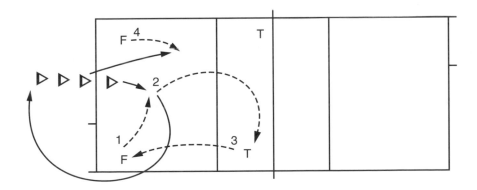

MOCK BLOCK AND SET

Purpose: To practice quick recovery from blocking to setting.

Procedure: The coach yells, "Block!" and the area 2 player jumps and then lands on the outside foot and pivots toward the coach to see where the ball is. The player moves to the ball, sets to area 4, and then follows the set to become the target player.

Key points: The coach should move all over the court and toss the ball so that the setter has to run, dive, roll, or sprawl to deliver the set. Occasionally the coach should be on the sideline in area 1 so that the setter can practice pivoting on the inside foot to look for the ball.

Equipment and personnel: A coach, three to six players, and one ball.

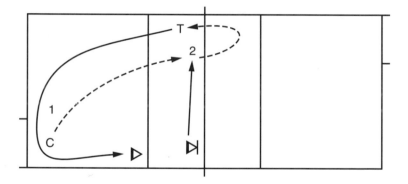

BLOCK AND SET

Purpose: To train players to keep their eyes open while blocking to determine which way to pivot to get to the ball and set.

Procedure: The coach yells, "Block!" and the area 2 player attempts to block as the coach spikes the ball at the area 1 digger. The blocker returns to the floor and sets the dug ball to the target player in area 4.

Key points: The starting setter should tilt the wrists and fingers back when blocking to "soft block" to prevent sprained or broken fingers. The soft block also speeds up the drill, as most spikes are deflected to the area 1 digger.

Equipment and personnel: A platform, a ball, a coach, a feeder, a digger, a blocker/setter, and a target player.

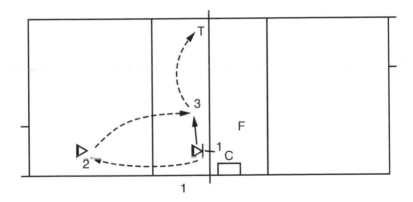

SPIKE OR JUMP SET

Purpose: To add diversity to the offense.

Procedure: The coach yells, "Block!" and the two players in area 2 mock block, then back off the net for an approach as the coach throws the ball to the area 2 hitter. The hitter has the option of spiking or setting to either of the frontcourt teammates, depending on the reaction of the opponent middle blocker.

Key point: The area 2 spiker should hit the ball when only one blocker opposes.

Equipment and personnel: Seven to 12 players; one ball.

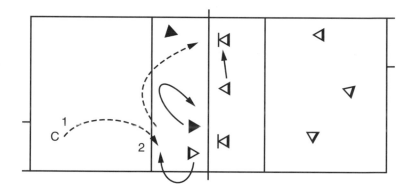

ATTACKING DRILLS

FOUR-STEP APPROACH

Purpose: To teach the players the best footwork to use when there is time for a long approach.

Procedure: The spiker lines up behind the three-meter line and steps on the tape the coach has placed on the court. The letter R (right foot) is taped for the first step, L (left foot) for the second, R for the third, and L for the final step. The steps increase in length from the first to the last step. The lengths of the steps depend on the age and size of the team members. Stronger and bigger players take larger steps. Use three lines on each court.

Key points: Players should increase their speed and use a two-foot takeoff with proper arm action and simulate the spike.

Equipment and personnel: Tape that does not remove varnish or paint; one coach for every court.

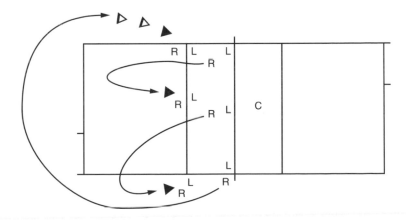

THREE-STEP APPROACH

Purpose: To teach players the best footwork to use when spiking a low outside set or when making quick transitions from defense to offense.

Procedure: The spiker lines up even with the three-meter line and uses a left-foot, right-foot approach. The coach creates a diagram on the floor with tape, and the spiker follows the diagram and simulates a spike without the ball.

Key points: The three-step approach should be used when receiving a low, fast set. An outside hitter who sees the setter receive a good pass should yell, "Go!", "Shoot!", or some other verbal signal to ensure a low, fast set to beat the middle blocker.

Equipment and personnel: Tape that does not remove varnish or paint; 1 to 12 players and one coach.

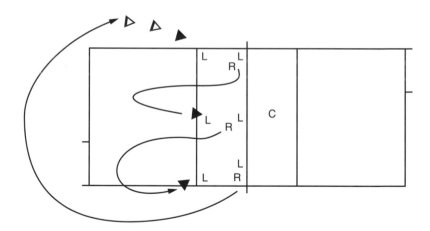

RAPID-FIRE SPIKING

Purpose: To warm up the players and allow them to work on whatever spiking position they desire against one blocker.

Procedure: Set up three spiking lines, with one setter and one blocker. First the area 2 spikes, then those in areas 3 and 4, pass the ball and spike in rapid order. The hitting sequence is left, middle, right, right, middle, left, left, middle, right. The blocker blocks nine times (three trips across the net) and then is replaced by a new blocker. The spikers shag their own spikes and return to a spiking line.

Key points: The coach can concentrate on watching the spikers' approaches to make sure they wait long enough after the pass to approach fast for a maximum jump. If they leave too soon, they will have to slow down for the set, which will decrease the jump.

Equipment and personnel: One ball for every spiker; 9 to 12 players to a court.

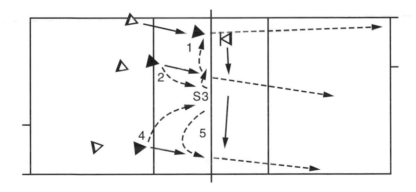

QUICK TRANSITION AUDIBLES

Purpose: To give the quick hitter practice in calling for sets in transition while building endurance.

Procedure: The coach throws the ball to the quick hitter, who passes to the setter and calls for a particular set, takes the proper route, and spikes the ball. The action is repeated for a specified number of sets, depending on the maturity and condition of the hitter. Ten spikes are a starting point for well-conditioned college players.

Key point: The shaggers should yell encouragement.

Equipment and personnel: Four shaggers, a feeder, a coach, one to four quick hitters, at least 10 balls, and a cart.

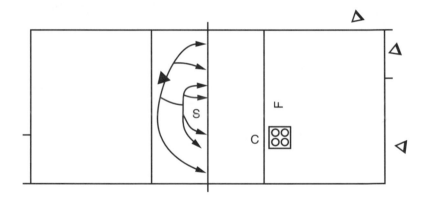

MOCK, BLOCK, AND SPIKE

Purpose: To speed up the spikers' transition from blocking to spiking.

Procedure: The coach calls, "Jump!" and the spiker blocks as the coach throws the ball to the middle back player to set. After the spike, the hitter quickly assumes the blocking position and the drill is repeated.

Key point: For endurance training, use 10 spikes apiece.

Equipment and personnel: Ten balls, a ball cart, one coach, and 5 to 12 players.

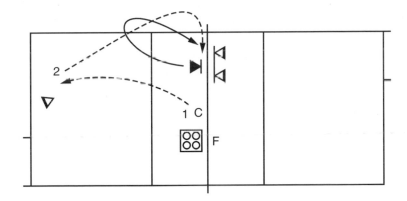

BLOCKING DRILLS

PARTNER BLOCKING

Purpose: To develop the blockers' movement technique and warm up before blocking.

Procedure: The blockers slide step across two nets and mock block three times along each net with their partners. This drill is done without a ball because the entire squad is involved. Players push against each other's hands on top of the net rather than the ball. After each player has slide stepped two courts to the left and right, the drill can be repeated using the crossover step.

Key point: Match up the players according to height and jumping ability so that everyone can use maximum block jumps to help increase power.

Equipment and personnel: Two courts and the entire squad.

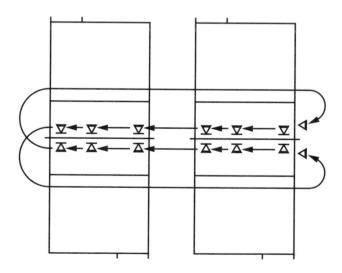

RAPID-FIRE BLOCKING

Purpose: To warm up the players for spiking and blocking and to improve these two techniques.

Procedure: One blocker faces three hitting lines and attempts to block the area 4, area 3, and area 2 hitters in rapid succession. The hitting sequence is left, middle, right, right, middle, left, left, middle, right. The spikers pass their own balls as soon as the setter delivers the previous set to keep the blocker moving; each blocker makes three trips across the front row until everyone blocks. The drill usually is repeated. The spikers shag their own balls and return to the hitting line of their choice.

Key points: The blocker should penetrate above the net *before* the spiker contacts the ball.

Equipment and personnel: All available courts; one ball for each spiker.

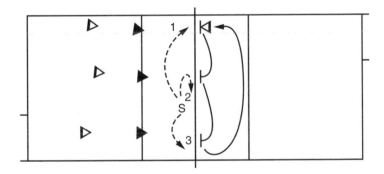

ONE-ON-ONE REPETITIVE BLOCKS

Purpose: To learn to watch the spiker's body and arm to read the direction of the spike.

Procedure: The coach stands on a platform and repetitively spikes balls down the line or crosscourt. The coach's body turns in the direction of the intended spike so that the blockers learn to position themselves according to the spiker's body line. The blocker rotates to the feeder and then to the shagger when the coach decides the player has had enough. Two drills can take place on the same court.

Key point: Watch the blocker's eyes to make sure they are open when the spiker contacts the ball.

Equipment and personnel: A platform, eight balls, a spiker, a blocker, a feeder, and a shagger or shaggers.

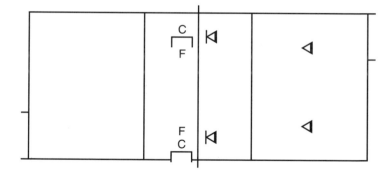

BLOCK AND ATTACK

Purpose: To block and approach to spike after blocking while building endurance.

Procedure: The coach stands on a platform and spikes balls at the blocker. After blocking, the player immediately backs off the net to spike a ball thrown by another coach or teammate, and the action is quickly repeated.

Key point: Vary the sets so that the attacker's range increases.

Equipment and personnel: A platform, 10 balls, four shaggers, two feeders, a coach, a setter, and a blocker/attacker.

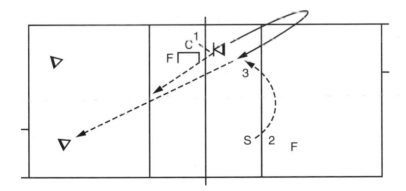

DIGGING DRILLS

THREE-PERSON PEPPER

Purpose: To allow the digger to use the court in a game situation by attempting to dig a spike to the setter at the net.

Procedure: The spiker stands in area 4, back to the net, and hits to the digger's area of responsibility. The digger directs the spiked ball to the setter, who jump-sets the ball to the spiker. The action is repeated until the ball hits the floor. Any of the three players can initiate the sequence.

Key points: If the beginning spiker cannot control the spike, the set may be caught and tossed and hit. Insist that the setter jump-set all good digs within the three-meter line. Jumpsets give the blocker less time to react and on many occasions take a blocker out of the play.

Equipment and personnel: One ball for every three players.

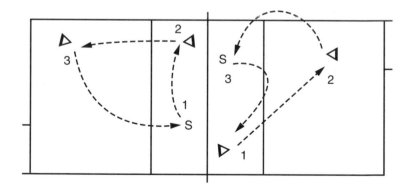

TWO-PERSON PEPPER

Purpose: To give the entire team an opportunity to dig and set using many repetitions in a short period of time. This drill is usually used in the beginning of a practice or prematch warm-up.

Procedure: Two players team up with one ball and stand about 20 feet apart. (A team of 12 could place six players on each side of the net.) Player A spikes to player B, who digs back to player A. Player A sets to B, who spikes to A, and the players continue to spike, dig, and set to each other.

Key points: The players should vary the placement of hard spikes and off-speed shots so that the defenders have to go to the floor to retrieve the shots. Some coaches prefer to have one partner, whose back is to the net, spike all the balls at the other partner, then have the two partners change places. The reason for this placement is to simulate game conditions so that the diggers will control the ball on their side of the net.

Equipment and personnel: One ball for every two players. (The entire squad may participate at the same time.)

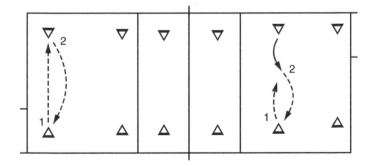

DOUBLES

Purpose: To stimulate movement and promote "quick feet."

Procedure: The coach stands on the sideline near the net and passes the ball to either of two attackers on the same side of the court; this pass counts for the first three contacts. The player receiving the pass must set the ball to a teammate, who attempts to put it away. If successful, the players rotate to the end of the line; if the defenders put the ball away, the attackers become the defenders. If the defenders lose to three attackers in a row, they are penalized and must perform 10 quick dives before the coach resumes the drill. The two defenders stay in until they beat the attackers.

Key point: When the defenders are too weak or unskilled to dive, substitute sprawls, rolls, or push-ups for the penalty.

Equipment and personnel: Three balls, 6 to 12 players, and a coach.

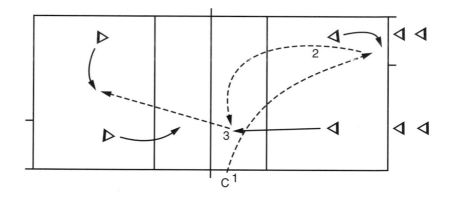

DIG AND SPIKE

Purpose: To train the area 4 spiker to dig and quickly approach to spike.

Procedure: The coach stands on a platform and spikes at the area 4 player, who digs the ball to the setter, positioned near the net between areas 2 and 3. After the dig the spiker swings toward the sideline for a wide set and tries to defeat two blockers. This is repeated for 10 trials; then the player rests for 10 trials and repeats the drill. Use up to three repetitions, depending on the condition of the players.

Key points: Use some dinks to area 3 to cause the spiker to dive and then get up quickly to run back to area 4 to spike. After a dive the setter may have to set higher than usual to give the player time to reach the assignment.

Equipment and personnel: A platform, six balls, a coach, a setter, two blockers, a spiker, and three to six shaggers.

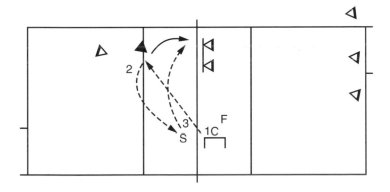

THE PIT

Purpose: To test the limits of a player's defensive capabilities.

Procedure: The digger is surrounded by peers who have just gone through or will go through the drill. The coach hits balls near the player in a rapid fashion, causing the player to dive, roll, sprawl, and grovel to dig everything possible. The object is to condition the player to attempt to dig every ball—not to make judgments, but to react quickly. The player's teammates shag and encourage the digger.

Key point: To extend the player's range, alternate balls spiked just out of range interspersed with balls within reach.

Equipment and personnel: Twelve balls, a coach, a feeder, and 6 to 12 players.

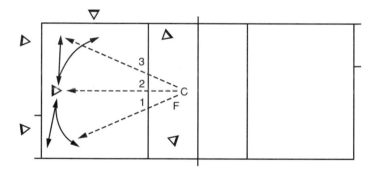

PURSUIT

Purpose: To extend the effective range of the entire defense.

Procedure: The coach stands on a platform and spikes a high flat ball off the blockers so that it travels out of bounds. The players pursue the ball so that the digger can pass the ball to someone nearby rather than try to pass the ball 30 feet to the nearest teammate.

Key points: To avoid injuries, do not allow play on adjoining courts during the drill. Players should try to set the ball to the frontcourt and score.

Equipment and personnel: A platform, a coach, six balls, two blockers, and six defenders.

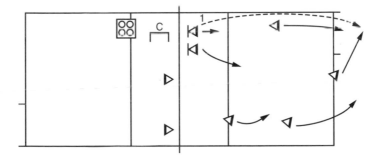

CHAPTER 7

YEAR-ROUND CONDITIONING

Long gone are the days of beginning workouts a month or so before preseason practice begins. These days, athletes must train year-round to attain superiority over opponents. That includes volleyball players. Whether your level of training is basic or advanced, your concentration must be on improving throughout the year. That means following a year-round workout program geared toward achieving maximum benefits at the right time.

A volleyball athlete's year-round training regimen can be divided into three 16-week phases: preparation, strength, and power. That leaves four weeks for rest, relaxation, and recreation. The cycle of exercises differs between the beginning and advanced levels, but all athletes should adhere to this schedule, starting with the first 16-week phase during the off-season and progressing to the strength and power phases. Exercises should be performed in the order presented.

BEGINNING AND ADVANCED CYCLES

Athletes with a limited amount of exposure to strength training should follow the beginner's program. During each 16-week phase (see tables 7.1 through 7.3), the athlete will work out two days a week. An advanced athlete is one who already has developed a solid strength base. Advanced athletes will work out three days a week during each 16-week phase (see tables 7.4 through 7.6).

Training schedules for beginning and advanced athletes are designed to be flexible to fit an athlete's schedule. For example, a beginner who works out two days a week can choose Monday and Wednesday, or perhaps Tuesday and Thursday—any two nonconsecutive days that fit into the athlete's schedule and can consistently be followed. An advanced athlete typically will work out on Monday, Wednesday, and Friday. Again, the program is meant to be flexible, and common sense should dictate. Every high school, college, or club team adheres to a different schedule, and athletes should tailor their personal workout routines around that schedule.

In the preparation phase, an athlete who has been idle for a period of time works gradually to become reaccustomed to a workout program. Rather than intensity, the emphasis is on high volume of repetitions and low weight. A good period of time is devoted to developing flexibility and proper form, strengthening tendons and ligaments, and conditioning muscles.

During the strength phase, reps are reduced and weight is increased, and the workout becomes more intense. The emphasis shifts to developing core strength.

During the power phase, reps are reduced even further and weight is increased even more. The emphasis shifts to working toward transferring some of the strength developed in the previous 16 weeks into functional power—things that can be applied on the volleyball court.

Periodization

With any workout program, the goal is to progress until maximum results are achieved at the best possible time. Athletes refer to this as *peaking*. A well-designed workout program will incorporate periodization, which is designed to allow an athlete to peak at a predetermined time. Usually, it is before the start of a season, a crucial game, or whatever point the coach or athlete decides. That means you want to be finishing the 16-week power phase when this point in time is approaching.

Properly structuring a workout program means developing optimum progression. Like placing building blocks carefully, an athlete builds a solid foundation with the goal of working toward a peak where maximum results are achieved.

Brook Rundle

Brooke Rundle heard it time and again while growing up: *You're good, but you're too small.* True, Rundle, a former setter for UC Santa Barbara, grew to only 5 feet, 6 inches—diminutive by comparison to most top-ranked volleyball players. But lack of size never deterred Rundle. It only motivated her. "Don't listen to anybody, I told her," said Larry Rundle, Brooke's father and a former UCLA and Team U.S.A. volleyball player. "Just do what you need to do."

Rundle proved her point by being selected as a second-team American Volleyball Coaches Association (AVCA) All-American as a junior in 2000. She also earned first-team All Big West Conference honors for the third consecutive year. Among 24 All-American selections, Rundle was among only two players shorter than 6 feet. That season, Rundle played in all 122 games and started all 34 matches for the Gauchos. Such durability is a tribute to her dedication to training and burning desire to succeed.

A well-organized program of weight training and plyometrics helped Rundle make the necessary strides toward a higher level of competition. Rundle spent countless hours performing jump exercises while carrying weights, duplicating the movements she made on the court. Her work paid off when she was selected Big West freshman of the year, leading the conference with 1,575 assists.

Ever the competitor, Rundle attracted a crowd while attending a camp at the University of Washington, where she challenged the school record for push-ups. Rundle shattered the women's mark of 65 and came within one of the men's record of 109. "Just because she was challenged to do it," Larry Rundle said. Rundle graduated from Santa Barbara in 2002 and is embarking on a professional playing career in Europe.

Technique Versus Tonnage

As with any weight program, it is important to perform each exercise correctly and safely. Just as the game of volleyball is very technique oriented, so is the practice of weightlifting among players. Technique should always be emphasized over tonnage, no matter how many times the lift is repeated. Over time, a player may begin to add increased weight, but with each increase a player must remain focused on perfecting technique.

Technique is important on the court and in the weightroom.

Christy Cochran

Christy Cochran, an outside hitter and former captain of the Penn State women's volleyball team, led the Nittany Lions to an undefeated regular season in 1998 and three final four appearances during a four-year career that defined dedication.

"Our goal each year is to compete for a national championship," longtime Nittany Lions head coach Russ Rose says. "Some years, you have a core group of players who are better able to do it than other years. They recognize the value of getting into the weight room and embrace the desire to get in shape."

Perhaps no one exemplified this philosophy better than Cochran, now an assistant coach at Texas, who led the Nittany Lions to a four-year record of 127-14 (.901). She is described by Rose as the "the hardest-working athlete" he has seen in 24 seasons as head coach at Penn State.

Cochran was a two-time all-district selection and a 1998 All-American selection by *Volleyball* magazine. Her commitment not only propelled her from tiny Bethlehem, Pennsylvania Catholic High School to national prominence, it rubbed off on players in and out of the Nittany Lions' gym.

Observers marveled at Cochran's well-conditioned physique, particularly her muscular legs, which rivaled those of a football player. Cochran's attitude toward weight training was infectious, motivating teammates and inspiring observers to inquire about her regimen.

"So many people used to write me letters about her," Rose says. "She was a dynamo. She decided that maybe her volleyball skills or her volleyball IQ weren't as strong as players who had played longer, but she honestly believed if she committed herself to training she could compete. She always said she didn't want to be Miss America, she wanted to be Miss Gladiator."

Cochran turned to coaching after a two-year professional career in Europe and the United States. In 2000-2001, she played in Oporto, Portugal, for Castelo da Maia, helping to win the Portuguese championship and advance to the round of 16 in the European Cup.

Posture and Breathing

Good technique begins with good posture. Before performing any lift, you must be properly *set*, with a flat or arched back, a tight abdomen, chest out, shoulders back, and head raised and level. Every lift requires you to achieve a specific set position before beginning the first rep.

Correct breathing also is essential with any exercise. Take a big breath before starting each rep, then exhale at the completion of the rep. Holding your breath helps to stabilize the trunk muscles, making it easier to hold the set position.

Range of Motion

Training should be done using a full range of motion for all exercises. The benefits are many. Pushed to their full range, muscles and tendons develop flexibility. Muscle fibers are stimulated and joints are stabilized. Injuries are less likely. If injury does occur, proper rehabilitation will lead to a return to full range of motion.

Equipment and Safety

Many athletes avoid certain types of training because they think they don't have the proper equipment or are uncertain about how to use it. Weight belts, knee wraps, and lifting suits are fine for bodybuilders, but most volleyball players have no need for them. Remember the emphasis on technique. Volleyball players who require belts or wraps are lifting too much weight. The goal is to achieve strength and balance. A player who has a history of lower back problems, however, or who simply feels more comfortable wearing a belt should not be discouraged from wearing one. In any case, you should use a spotter for safety.

Table 7.1   Beginner Preparation Cycle

For athletes with no exposure to strength training. This cycle focuses on building core strength and body balance.

Day 1	Wk 1	Wk 2	Wk 3	Wk 4	Wk 5	Wk 6	Wk 7	Wk 8
Exercise	Number of reps							
Body weight lunges	2×8	3×6	2×10	3×8	2×12	3×10	2×15	3×12
Push-ups	10	15	20	25	30	35	40	Off
Pull-ups	5	8	10	12	15	18	20	Off
Dips	5	8	10	12	15	18	20	Off
Crunches	25	35	45	55	65	75	85	Off
Supermans	12	18	22	28	32	38	42	Off

Day 1	Wk 9	Wk 10	Wk 11	Wk 12	Wk 13	Wk 14	Wk 15	Wk 16
Exercise	Number of reps							
Body weight lunges	Off	3×8	4×6	3×10	4×8	3×12	4×10	3×15
Push-ups	2×max	3×max	2×max	2×max	3×max	2×max	3×max	3×max
Pull-ups	2×max	2×max	3×max	2×max	3×max	3×max	2×max	3×max
Dips	2×max	2×max	2×max	3×max	2×max	3×max	3×max	3×max
Crunches	85	95	105	115	125	135	145	150
Supermans	42	48	52	58	62	68	72	75

(continued)

Table 7.1   Beginner Preparation Cycle *(continued)*

Day 2	Wk 1	Wk 2	Wk 3	Wk 4	Wk 5	Wk 6	Wk 7	Wk 8
Exercise	Number of reps							
Body weight squats	3×6	2×10	3×8	2×12	3×10	2×15	3×12	2×20
Push-ups	5	8	10	12	15	18	20	Off
Pull-ups	10	15	20	25	30	35	40	Off
Dips	5	8	10	12	15	18	20	Off
Crunches	40	50	60	70	80	90	100	Off
Supermans	20	25	30	35	40	45	50	Off

Day 2	Wk 9	Wk 10	Wk 11	Wk 12	Wk 13	Wk 14	Wk 15	Wk 16
Exercise	Number of reps							
Body weight squats	Off	4×6	3×10	4×8	3×12	4×10	3×15	4×12
Push-ups	2× max	2× max	3× max	2× max	2× max	3× max	2× max	3× max
Pull-ups	2× max	3× max	2× max	3× max	3× max	3× max	3× max	3× max
Dips	2× max	2× max	2× max	2× max	3× max	2× max	3× max	3× max
Crunches	90	100	110	120	130	140	150	150
Supermans	45	50	55	60	65	70	75	75

Table 7.2   Beginner Strength Cycle

For athletes with no exposure to strength training. This cycle
focuses on building core strength.

Day 1	Wk 1	Wk 2	Wk 3	Wk 4	Wk 5	Wk 6	Wk 7	Wk 8
Exercise	Number of reps							
Dumbbell lunges	4×8 lite	3×12 lite	4×10 lite	3×15 lite	4×8 +wt	4×8 +wt	4×8 +wt	Off
Bench press	4×8 lite	3×12 lite	4×10 lite	3×15 lite	4×8 +wt	4×8 +wt	4×8 +wt	Off
Dumbbell bent row	3×6	3×8	3×10	3×12	3×15	3×15	3×15	Off
Triceps push-down	2×8	2×10	2×12	2×15	2×15	2×15	2×15	Off
Regular abs	25	35	45	55	65	75	85	Off
Russian twist	20	25	30	35	40	45	50	Off
Body weight rev. hyper-extension	3×6	3×8	3×10	3×12	3×15	3×15	3×15	Off

Day 1	Wk 9	Wk 10	Wk 11	Wk 12	Wk 13	Wk 14	Wk 15	Wk 16
Exercise	Number of reps							
Dumbbell lunges	4×6 lite	4×6 +wt	4×6 +wt	5×5 lite	5×5 +wt	5×5 +wt	5×4 lite	5×4 +wt
Bench press	4×6 lite	4×6 +wt	4×6 +wt	5×5 lite	5×5 +wt	5×5 +wt	5×4 lite	5×4 +wt
Dumbbell bent row	3×12 lite	3×12 +wt	3×12 +wt	3×10 lite	3×10 +wt	3×10 +wt	4×8 lite	4×8 +wt
Triceps push-down	2×12 lite	2×12 +wt	2×12 +wt	2×10 lite	2×10 +wt	2×10 +wt	3×8 lite	3×8 +wt
Regular abs	85	95	105	115	125	135	145	150
Russian twist	45	50	55	60	65	70	75	75
Body weight rev. hyper-extension	3×12	3×12	3×12	3×10	3×10	3×10	4×8	4×8

(continued)

Table 7.2   Beginner Strength Cycle *(continued)*

Day 2	Wk 1	Wk 2	Wk 3	Wk 4	Wk 5	Wk 6	Wk 7	Wk 8
Exercise	Number of reps							
Front squat	4×8 lite	3×12 lite	4×10 lite	3×15 lite	4×8 +wt	4×8 +wt	4×8 +wt	Off
Military press	4×8 lite	3×12 lite	4×10 lite	3×15 lite	4×8 +wt	4×8 +wt	4×8 +wt	Off
Lat pull down	3×6	3×8	3×10	3×12	3×15	3×15	3×15	Off
Lying triceps	2×8	2×10	2×12	2×15	2×15	2×15	2×15	Off
Regular abs	25	35	45	55	65	75	85	Off
Russian twist	20	25	30	35	40	45	50	Off
Body weight rev. hyper-extension	3×6	3×8	3×10	3×12	3×15	3×15	3×15	Off

Day 2	Wk 9	Wk 10	Wk 11	Wk 12	Wk 13	Wk 14	Wk 15	Wk 16
Exercise	Number of reps							
Front squat	4×6 lite	4×6 +wt	4×6 +wt	5×5 lite	5×5 +wt	5×5 +wt	5×4 lite	5×4 +wt
Military press	4×6 lite	4×6 +wt	4×6 +wt	5×5 lite	5×5 +wt	5×5 +wt	5×4 lite	5×4 +wt
Lat pull down	3×12 lite	3×12 +wt	3×12 +wt	3×10 lite	3×10 +wt	3×10 +wt	4×8 lite	4×8 +wt
Lying triceps	2×12 lite	2×12 +wt	2×12 +wt	2×10 lite	2×10 +wt	2×10 +wt	3×8 lite	3×8 +wt
Regular abs	85	95	105	115	125	135	145	150
Russian twist	45	50	55	60	65	70	75	75
Body weight rev. hyper-extension	3×12	3×12	3×12	3×10	3×10	3×10	4×8	4×8

Table 7.3 Beginner Power Cycle

This cycle focuses on transitioning core strength into functional power.

Day 1	Wk 1	Wk 2	Wk 3	Wk 4	Wk 5	Wk 6	Wk 7	Wk 8
Exercise	Number of reps							
Scissor jumps	6×2	8×2	10×2	6×4	6×6	8×4	8×6	Off
Barbell lunges	4×6 lite	4×6 +wt	4×6 +wt	5×5 lite	5×5 +wt	5×5 +wt	5×4 lite	Off
Bench press	4×6 lite	4×6 +wt	4×6 +wt	5×5 lite	5×5 +wt	5×5 +wt	5×4 lite	Off
Dumbbell bent row	3×10 lite	3×10 +wt	3×10 +wt	4×8 lite	4×8 +wt	4×8 +wt	3×10 lite	Off
Triceps push-down	2×10 lite	2×10 +wt	2×10 +wt	3×8 lite	3×8 +wt	2×10 lite	3×8 +wt	Off
Cardinal abs	25	35	45	55	65	75	85	Off
Weighted russian twist	20	25	30	35	40	45	50	Off
Weighted rev. hyper-extension	3×12	3×12	3×12	3×10	3×10	3×10	4×8	Off

Day 1	Wk 9	Wk 10	Wk 11	Wk 12	Wk 13	Wk 14	Wk 15	Wk 16
Exercise	Number of reps							
Scissor jumps	6×6	8×6	8×6	6×6	8×6	6×6	8×6	6×6
Barbell lunges	4×5 lite	5×4 +wt	4×5 lite	5×4 +wt	4×5 lite	5×4 +wt	4×5 lite	5×4 +wt
Bench press	5×4 +wt	4×5 lite	5×4 +wt	4×5 lite	5×4 +wt	4×5 lite	5×4 +wt	4×5 lite
Dumbbell bent row	4×8 +wt	3×10 lite	4×8 +wt	3×10 lite	4×8 +wt	3×10 lite	4×8 +wt	3×10 lite
Triceps push-down	2×10 lite	3×8 +wt	2×10 lite	3×8 +wt	2×10 lite	3×8 +wt	2×10 lite	3×8 +wt
Cardinal abs	85	95	105	115	125	135	145	150
Weighted russian twist	45	50	55	60	65	70	75	75
Weighted rev. hyper-extension	3×10	3×10	3×10	4×8	4×8 +wt	4×8 +wt	4×8 +wt	4×8 +wt

(continued)

Table 7.3   Beginner Power Cycle *(continued)*

Day 2	Wk 1	Wk 2	Wk 3	Wk 4	Wk 5	Wk 6	Wk 7	Wk 8
Exercise	Number of reps							
Tuck jumps	6×2	8×2	10×2	6×4	6×6	8×4	8×6	Off
Front squat	4×6 lite	4×6 +wt	4×6 +wt	5×5 lite	5×5 +wt	5×5 +wt	5×4 lite	Off
Military press	4×6 lite	4×6 +wt	4×6 +wt	5×5 lite	5×5 +wt	5×5 +wt	5×4 lite	Off
Lat pull-down	3×10 lite	3×10 +wt	3×10 +wt	4×8 lite	4×8 +wt	4×8 +wt	3×10 lite	Off
Lying triceps	2×10 lite	2×10 +wt	2×10 +wt	3×8 lite	3×8 +wt	2×10 lite	3×8 +wt	Off
Cardinal abs	25	35	45	55	65	75	85	Off
Weighted russian twist	20	25	30	35	40	45	50	Off
Weighted rev. hyper-extension	3×12	3×12	3×12	3×10	3×10	3×10	4×8	Off

Day 2	Wk 9	Wk 10	Wk 11	Wk 12	Wk 13	Wk 14	Wk 15	Wk 16
Exercise	Number of reps							
Tuck jumps	6×6	8×6	6×6	8×6	6×6	8×6	6×6	8×6
Front squat	5×4 +wt	4×5 lite	5×4 +wt	4×5 lite	5×4 +wt	4×5 lite	5×4 +wt	4×5 lite
Military press	4×5 lite	5×4 +wt	4×5 lite	5×4 +wt	4×5 lite	5×4 +wt	4×5 lite	5×4 +wt
Lat pull-down	3×10 lite	4×8 +wt	3×10 lite	4×8 +wt	3×10 lite	4×8 +wt	3×10 lite	4×8 +wt
Lying triceps	3×8 +wt	2×10 lite	3×8 +wt	2×10 lite	3×8 +wt	2×10 lite	3×8 +wt	2×10 lite
Cardinal abs	85	95	105	115	125	135	145	150
Weighted russian twist	45	50	55	60	65	70	75	75
Weighted rev. hyper-extension	3×10	3×10	3×10	4×8	4×8 +wt	4×8 +wt	4×8 +wt	4×8 +wt

Table 7.4   Advanced Preparation Cycle

For athletes with sound base strength. This cycle focuses on building core strength and body balance.

Day 1	Wk 1	Wk 2	Wk 3	Wk 4	Wk 5	Wk 6	Wk 7	Wk 8
Exercise	Number of reps							
Scissor jumps	6×4	6×6	6×8	6×10	8×4	8×6	8×8	Off
Hang clean	3×5 lite	4×5 lite	5×5 lite	5×5 +wt	5×5 +wt	5×5 +wt	5×5 +wt	Off
Snatch squat	2×8 lite	3×8 lite	4×8 lite	4×8 +wt	4×8 lite	4×8 lite	4×8 +wt	Off
Bench press	2×8 lite	3×8 lite	4×8 lite	4×8 +wt	4×8 +wt	4×8 +wt	4×8 +wt	Off
Bent row	2×8 lite	3×8 lite	4×8 lite	4×8 +wt	4×8 +wt	4×8 +wt	4×8 +wt	Off
Shoulder circuit	2×6 lite	3×6 lite	4×6 lite	4×6 lite	4×6 lite	4×6 lite	4×6 lite	Off
Cardinal abs	25	35	45	55	65	75	85	Off
Weighted russian twist	20	25	30	35	40	45	50	Off

Day 1	Wk 9	Wk 10	Wk 11	Wk 12	Wk 13	Wk 14	Wk 15	Wk 16
Exercise	Number of reps							
Scissor jumps	10×12	10×4	10×6	10×2	10×4	10×6	10×4	10×6
Hang clean	5×5 lite	5×5 +wt	5×5 lite	5×5 +wt	5×5 lite	5×5 +wt	5×5 lite	5×5 +wt
Snatch squat	4×8 lite	4×8 lite	4×8 +wt	4×8 lite	4×8 +wt	4×8 lite	4×8 +wt	4×8 lite
Bench press	4×8 lite	4×8 +wt	4×8 lite	4×8 lite	4×8 +wt	4×8 +wt	4×8 lite	4×8 lite
Bent row	4×8 lite	4×8 lite	4×8 +wt	4×8 +wt	4×8 lite	4×8 lite	4×8 +wt	4×8 +wt
Shoulder circuit	3×6 lite	4×6 lite	3×6 +wt	4×6 lite	4×6 lite	3×6 +wt	4×6 lite	4×6 lite
Cardinal abs	85	95	105	115	125	135	145	150
Weighted russian twist	45	50	55	60	65	70	75	75

(continued)

Table 7.4   Advanced Preparation Cycle *(continued)*

Day 2	Wk 1	Wk 2	Wk 3	Wk 4	Wk 5	Wk 6	Wk 7	Wk 8
Exercise	Number of reps							
Tuck jumps	6×4	6×6	6×8	6×10	8×4	8×6	8×8	Off
Hang snatch	3×5 lite	4×5 lite	5×5 lite	5×5 +wt	5×5 +wt	5×5 +wt	5×5 +wt	Off
Front squat	2×8 lite	3×8 lite	4×8 lite	4×8 lite	4×8 +wt	4×8 +wt	4×8 +wt	Off
Incline press	2×8 lite	3×8 lite	4×8 lite	4×8 +wt	4×8 +wt	4×8 +wt	4×8 +wt	Off
Lat pull-down	2×8 lite	3×8 lite	4×8 lite	4×8 +wt	4×8 +wt	4×8 +wt	4×8 +wt	Off
Weighted rev. hyper-extension	2×8 lite	3×8 lite	4×8 lite	4×8 lite	4×8 +wt	4×8 +wt	4×8 +wt	Off
Shoulder circuit	2×6 lite	3×6 lite	4×6 lite	4×6 lite	4×6 lite	4×6 lite	4×6 lite	Off
Cardinal abs	25	35	45	55	65	75	85	Off
Weighted russian twist	20	25	30	35	40	45	50	Off

Day 2	Wk 9	Wk 10	Wk 11	Wk 12	Wk 13	Wk 14	Wk 15	Wk 16
Exercise	Number of reps							
Tuck jumps	10×6	10×4	10×2	10×6	10×4	10×6	10×6	10×4
Hang snatch	5×5 lite	5×5 lite	5×5 +wt	5×5 lite	5×5 +wt	5×5 lite	5×5 +wt	5×5 lite
Front squat	4×8 lite	4×8 +wt	4×8 lite	4×8 +wt	4×8 lite	4×8 +wt	4×8 lite	4×8 +wt
Incline press	4×8 lite	4×8 lite	4×8 +wt	4×8 +wt	4×8 +wt	4×8 lite	4×8 +wt	4×8 +wt
Lat pull-down	4×8 lite	4×8 +wt	4×8 lite	4×8 lite	4×8 lite	4×8 +wt	4×8 lite	4×8 lite
Weighted rev. hyper-extension	4×8 lite	4×8 lite	4×8 +wt	4×8 lite	4×8 +wt	4×8 lite	4×8 +wt	4×8 lite
Shoulder circuit	3×6 lite	3×6 +wt	4×6 lite	4×6 lite	3×6 +wt	4×6 lite	4×6 lite	3×6 +wt
Cardinal abs	85	95	105	115	125	135	145	150
Weighted russian twist	45	50	55	60	65	70	75	75

(continued)

Table 7.4   Advanced Preparation Cycle *(continued)*

Day 3	Wk 1	Wk 2	Wk 3	Wk 4	Wk 5	Wk 6	Wk 7	Wk 8
Exercise	Number of reps							
Lateral cone hops	6×4	6×6	6×8	6×10	8×4	8×6	8×8	Off
Back squat	2×8 lite	3×8 lite	4×8 lite	4×8 +wt	4×8 lite	4×8 +wt	4×8 +wt	Off
Romanian dead lift	2×8 lite	3×8 lite	4×8 lite	4×8 lite	4×8 +wt	4×8 lite	4×8 +wt	Off
Military press	2×8 lite	3×8 lite	4×8 lite	4×8 +wt	4×8 +wt	4×8 +wt	4×8 +wt	Off
Pull-ups	1× max	2× max	3× max	3× max	3× max	3× max	3× max	Off
Shoulder circuit	2×6 lite	3×6 lite	4×6 lite	4×6 lite	4×6 lite	4×6 lite	4×6 lite	Off
Cardinal abs	25	35	45	55	65	75	85	Off
Weighted russian twist	20	25	30	35	40	45	50	Off

Day 3	Wk 9	Wk 10	Wk 11	Wk 12	Wk 13	Wk 14	Wk 15	Wk 16
Exercise	Number of reps							
Lateral cone hops	10×6	10×4	10×6	10×4	10×6	10×4	10×6	10×4
Back squat	4×8 lite	4×8 lite	4×8 +wt	4×8 lite	4×8 +wt	4×8 lite	4×8 +wt	4×8 lite
Romanian dead lift	4×8 lite	4×8 +wt	4×8 lite	4×8 +wt	4×8 lite	4×8 +wt	4×8 lite	4×8 +wt
Military press	4×8 lite	4×8 +wt	4×8 lite	4×8 +wt	4×8 +wt	4×8 +wt	4×8 lite	4×8 +wt
Pull-ups	2× max	3× max	3× max	3× max	3× max	3× max	3× max	Off
Shoulder circuit	3×6 lite	4×6 lite	4×6 lite	3×6 +wt	4×6 lite	4×6 lite	3×6 +wt	4×6 lite
Cardinal abs	85	95	105	115	125	135	145	150
Weighted russian twist	45	50	55	60	65	70	75	75

Table 7.5   Advanced Strength Cycle

This cycle focuses on building core strength.

Day 1	Wk 1	Wk 2	Wk 3	Wk 4	Wk 5	Wk 6	Wk 7	Wk 8
Exercise	Number of reps							
Scissor jump	12×2	12×4	12×6	10×4	10×6	12×2	12×4	Off
Hang clean	4×5 lite	5×5 lite	5×5 +wt	5×5 +wt	5×5 +wt	5×5 +wt	5×5 +wt	Off
Snatch squat	3×6 lite	4×6 lite	4×6 +wt	4×6 lite	4×6 lite	4×6 +wt	4×6 +wt	Off
Bench press	3×6 lite	4×6 lite	4×6 +wt	4×6 +wt	4×6 +wt	4×6 +wt	4×6 +wt	Off
Bent row	3×8 lite	4×8 lite	4×8 +wt	4×8 +wt	4×8 +wt	4×8 +wt	4×8 +wt	Off
Shoulder circuit	2×6 lite	3×6 lite	4×6 lite	4×6 lite	4×6 lite	4×6 lite	4×6 lite	Off
Cardinal abs	25	35	45	55	65	75	85	Off
Weighted russian twist	20	25	30	35	40	45	50	Off

Day 1	Wk 9	Wk 10	Wk 11	Wk 12	Wk 13	Wk 14	Wk 15	Wk 16
Exercise	Number of reps							
Scissor jump	10×2	10×4	10×6	12×2	12×4	12×3	12×2	10×2
Hang clean	5×4 lite	5×4 +wt	5×4 lite	5×4 +wt	5×4 lite	5×4 +wt	5×4 lite	5×4 +wt
Snatch squat	5×5 lite	4×4 lite	5×5 +wt	4×5 lite	5×4 +wt	4×5 lite	5×5 +wt	4×5 lite
Bench press	5×5 lite	5×5 +wt	4×5 lite	4×5 lite	5×5 +wt	5×5 +wt	4×5 lite	4×5 lite
Bent row	4×8 lite	4×8 lite	4×8 +wt	4×8 +wt	4×8 lite	4×8 lite	4×8 +wt	4×8 +wt
Shoulder circuit	3×6 lite	4×6 lite	3×6 +wt	4×6 lite	4×6 lite	3×6 +wt	4×6 lite	4×6 lite
Cardinal abs	85	95	105	115	125	135	145	150
Weighted russian twist	45	50	55	60	65	70	75	75

(continued)

Table 7.5 Advanced Strength Cycle *(continued)*

Day 2	Wk 1	Wk 2	Wk 3	Wk 4	Wk 5	Wk 6	Wk 7	Wk 8
Exercise	Number of reps							
Box jump	×8	×10	×12	×14	×16	×18	×20	Off
Hang snatch	4×5 lite	5×5 lite	5×5 +wt	5×5 +wt	5×5 +wt	5×5 +wt	5×5 +wt	Off
Front squat	3×6 lite	4×6 lite	4×6 lite	4×6 +wt	4×6 +wt	4×6 +wt	4×6 +wt	Off
Incline press	3×6 lite	4×6 lite	4×6 +wt	4×6 +wt	4×6 +wt	4×6 +wt	4×6 +wt	Off
Lat pull-down	3×8 lite	4×8 lite	4×8 +wt	4×8 +wt	4×8 +wt	4×8 +wt	4×8 +wt	Off
Weighted rev. hyper-extension	2×8 lite	3×8 lite	4×8 lite	4×8 lite	4×8 +wt	4×8 +wt	4×8 +wt	Off
Shoulder circuit	2×6 lite	3×6 lite	4×6 lite	4×6 lite	4×6 lite	4×6 lite	4×6 lite	Off
Medicine ball long throws	10	15	20	25	30	35	40	Off
Weighted russian twist	20	25	30	35	40	45	50	Off

Table 7.5   Advanced Strength Cycle *(continued)*

Day 2	Wk 9	Wk 10	Wk 11	Wk 12	Wk 13	Wk 14	Wk 15	Wk 16
Exercise	Number of reps							
Box jump	×10	×12	×14	×16	×18	×20	×25	×10
Hang snatch	5×4 lite	5×4 lite	5×4 +wt	5×4 lite	5×4 +wt	5×4 lite	5×4 +wt	5×4 lite
Front squat	4×5 lite	5×5 +wt	4×5 lite	5×5 +wt	4×5 lite	4×5 +wt	5×5 lite	4×5 +wt
Incline press	4×5 lite	4×5 lite	5×5 +wt	5×5 +wt	5×5 +wt	4×5 lite	5×5 +wt	5×5 +wt
Lat pull-down	4×8 lite	4×8 +wt	4×8 lite	4×8 lite	4×8 lite	4×8 +wt	4×8 lite	4×8 lite
Weighted rev. hyper-extension	4×8 lite	4×8 lite	4×8 +wt	4×8 lite	4×8 +wt	4×8 lite	4×8 +wt	4×8 lite
Shoulder circuit	3×6 lite	3×6 +wt	4×6 lite	4×6 lite	3×6 +wt	4×6 lite	4×6 lite	3×6 +wt
Medicine ball long throws	20	25	30	35	40	45	50	50
Weighted russian twist	45	50	55	60	65	70	75	75

(continued)

Table 7.5   Advanced Strength Cycle *(continued)*

Day 3	Wk 1	Wk 2	Wk 3	Wk 4	Wk 5	Wk 6	Wk 7	Wk 8
Exercise	Number of reps							
Lateral box jumps	6×4	6×6	6×8	6×10	8×4	8×6	8×8	Off
Back squat	4×6 lite	4×6 lite	4×6 +wt	4×6 lite	4×6 +wt	4×6 +wt	4×6 +wt	Off
Romanian dead lift	2×10 lite	3×10 lite	3×10 lite	3×10 lite	3×10 +wt	3×10 lite	3×10 +wt	Off
Military press	3×8 lite	4×8 lite	4×8 +wt	4×8 +wt	4×8 +wt	4×8 +wt	4×8 +wt	Off
Pull-ups	2× max	3× max	3× max	3× max	3× max	3× max	3× max	Off
Shoulder circuit	2×6 lite	3×6 lite	4×6 lite	4×6 lite	4×6 lite	4×6 lite	4×6 lite	Off
Cardinal abs	25	35	45	55	65	75	85	Off
Weighted russian twist	20	25	30	35	40	45	50	Off

Day 3	Wk 9	Wk 10	Wk 11	Wk 12	Wk 13	Wk 14	Wk 15	Wk 16
Exercise	Number of reps							
Lateral box jumps	10×6	10×4	10×6	10×4	10×6	10×4	10×6	10×4
Back squat	4×5 lite	4×5 lite	5×5 +wt	4×5 lite	5×5 +wt	4×5 lite	5×5 +wt	4×5 lite
Romanian dead lift	3×10 lite	3×10 +wt	3×10 lite	3×10 +wt	3×10 lite	3×10 +wt	3×10 lite	3×10 +wt
Military press	4×6 lite	4×6 +wt	4×6 lite	4×6 +wt	4×6 +wt	4×6 +wt	4×6 lite	4×6 +wt
Pull-ups	2× max	3× max	3× max	3× max	3× max	3× max	3× max	3× max
Shoulder circuit	3×6 lite	4×6 lite	4×6 lite	3×6 +wt	4×6 lite	4×6 lite	3×6 +wt	4×6 lite
Cardinal abs	85	95	105	115	125	135	145	150
Weighted russian twist	45	50	55	60	65	70	75	75

Table 7.6   Advanced Power Cycle

For athletes with sound base strength. This cycle focuses on transitioning core strength into functional power.

Day 1	Wk 1	Wk 2	Wk 3	Wk 4	Wk 5	Wk 6	Wk 7	Wk 8
Exercise	Number of reps							
Single leg box jump	×6	×8	×10	×12	×14	×16	×16	Off
Hang clean	4×4 lite	5×4 lite	5×4 +wt	5×4 +wt	5×4 +wt	5×4 +wt	5×4 +wt	Off
Explosive Romanian dead lift	3×6 lite	4×6 lite	4×6 +wt	4×6 +wt	4×6 +wt	4×6 +wt	4×6 +wt	Off
Bench press	3×5 lite	4×5 lite	5×5 +wt	5×5 +wt	5×5 +wt	5×4 +wt	5×5 +wt	Off
Bent row	3×6 lite	4×8 lite	4×8 +wt	4×8 +wt	4×8 +wt	4×8 +wt	4×8 +wt	Off
Shoulder circuit	2×6 lite	3×6 lite	4×6 lite	4×6 lite	4×6 lite	4×6 lite	4×6 lite	Off
Medicine ball long throws	10	15	20	25	30	35	40	Off
Weighted russian twist	20	25	30	35	40	45	50	Off

(continued)

Table 7.6 Advanced Power Cycle *(continued)*

Day 1	Wk 9	Wk 10	Wk 11	Wk 12	Wk 13	Wk 14	Wk 15	Wk 16
Exercise	Number of reps							
Single leg box jump	×12	×16	×14	×10	×12	×16	×14	×10
Hang clean	5×3 lite	5×3 +wt	5×3 lite	5×3 +wt	5×3 lite	5×3 +wt	5×3 lite	5×3 +wt
Explosive Romanian dead lift	4×5 lite	4×5 lite	4×5 +wt	4×5 lite	4×5 +wt	4×5 lite	4×5 +wt	4×5 lite
Bench press	4×6 lite	5×4 +wt	4×6 lite	4×6 lite	5×4 +wt	5×4 +wt	4×6 lite	4×6 lite
Bent row	4×8 lite	4×8 lite	4×8 +wt	4×8 +wt	4×8 lite	4×8 lite	4×8 +wt	4×8 +wt
Shoulder circuit	3×6 lite	4×6 lite	3×6 +wt	4×6 lite	4×6 lite	3×6 +wt	4×6 lite	4×6 lite
Medicine ball long throws	20	25	30	35	40	45	50	50
Weighted russian twist	45	50	55	60	65	70	75	75

Table 7.6   Advanced Power Cycle *(continued)*

Day 2	Wk 1	Wk 2	Wk 3	Wk 4	Wk 5	Wk 6	Wk 7	Wk 8
Exercise	Number of reps							
Depth jump	$\times$6	$\times$8	$\times$10	$\times$12	$\times$14	$\times$16	$\times$16	Off
Hang snatch	4$\times$4 lite	5$\times$4 lite	5$\times$4 +wt	5$\times$4 +wt	5$\times$4 +wt	5$\times$4 +wt	5$\times$4 +wt	Off
Front squat	3$\times$5 lite	4$\times$5 lite	4$\times$5 lite	5$\times$5 +wt	4$\times$5 +wt	5$\times$5 +wt	4$\times$5 +wt	Off
Incline press	3$\times$5 lite	4$\times$5 lite	5$\times$5 +wt	4$\times$5 +wt	5$\times$5 +wt	4$\times$5 +wt	5$\times$5 +wt	Off
Lat pull-down	3$\times$8 lite	4$\times$8 lite	4$\times$8 +wt	4$\times$8 +wt	4$\times$8 +wt	4$\times$8 +wt	4$\times$8 +wt	Off
Weighted rev. hyper-extension	2$\times$8 lite	3$\times$8 lite	4$\times$8 lite	4$\times$8 lite	4$\times$8 +wt	4$\times$8 +wt	4$\times$8 +wt	Off
Shoulder circuit	2$\times$6 lite	3$\times$6 lite	4$\times$6 lite	4$\times$6 lite	4$\times$6 lite	4$\times$6 lite	4$\times$6 lite	Off
Cardinal abs	25	35	45	55	65	75	85	Off
Weighted russian twist	20	25	30	35	40	45	50	Off

(continued)

Table 7.6 Advanced Power Cycle *(continued)*

Day 2	Wk 9	Wk 10	Wk 11	Wk 12	Wk 13	Wk 14	Wk 15	Wk 16
Exercise	Number of reps							
Depth jump	×12	×14	×16	×18	×20	×20	×20	×16
Hang snatch	5×3 lite	5×3 lite	5×3 +wt	5×3 lite	5×3 +wt	5×3 lite	5×3 +wt	5×3 lite
Front squat	4×6 lite	5×4 +wt	4×6 lite	5×4 +wt	4×6 lite	5×4 +wt	4×6 lite	5×4 +wt
Incline press	4×6 lite	4×6 lite	5×4 +wt	5×4 +wt	5×4 +wt	4×6 lite	5×4 +wt	5×4 +wt
Lat pull-down	4×8 lite	4×8 +wt	4×8 lite	4×8 lite	4×8 lite	4×8 +wt	4×8 lite	4×8 lite
Weighted rev. hyper-extension	4×8 lite	4×8 lite	4×8 +wt	4×8 lite	4×8 +wt	4×8 lite	4×8 +wt	4×8 lite
Shoulder circuit	3×6 lite	3×6 +wt	4×6 lite	4×6 lite	3×6 +wt	4×6 lite	4×6 lite	3×6 +wt
Cardinal abs	85	95	105	115	125	135	145	150
Weighted russian twist	45	50	55	60	65	70	75	75

Table 7.6   Advanced Power Cycle *(continued)*

Day 3	Wk 1	Wk 2	Wk 3	Wk 4	Wk 5	Wk 6	Wk 7	Wk 8
Exercise	Number of reps							
Lateral box jumps	6×4	6×6	6×8	6×10	8×4	8×6	8×8	Off
Explosive back squat	3×6 lite	4×6 lite	4×6 +wt	4×6 lite	4×6 +wt	4×6 +wt	4×6 +wt	Off
Push press	3×6 lite	4×6 lite	4×6 +wt	4×6 +wt	4×6 +wt	4×6 +wt	4×6 +wt	Off
Pull-ups	2× max	3× max	3× max	3× max	3× max	3× max	3× max	Off
Shoulder circuit	2×6 lite	3×6 lite	4×6 lite	4×6 lite	4×6 lite	4×6 lite	4×6 lite	Off
Medicine ball long throws	10	15	20	25	30	35	40	Off
Weighted russian twist	20	25	30	35	40	45	50	Off

Day 3	Wk 9	Wk 10	Wk 11	Wk 12	Wk 13	Wk 14	Wk 15	Wk 16
Exercise	Number of reps							
Lateral box jumps	10×6	10×4	10×6	10×4	10×6	10×4	10×6	10×4
Explosive back squat	5×5 lite	5×5 lite	5×5 +wt	5×5 lite	5×5 +wt	5×5 lite	5×5 +wt	5×5 lite
Push press	5×5 lite	5×5 +wt	5×5 lite	5×5 +wt	5×5 +wt	5×5 +wt	5×5 lite	5×5 +wt
Pull-ups	2× max	3× max	3× max	3× max	3× max	3× max	3× max	3× max
Shoulder circuit	3×6 lite	4×6 lite	4×6 lite	3×6 +wt	4×6 lite	4×6 lite	3×6 +wt	4×6 lite
Medicine ball long throws	20	25	30	35	40	45	50	50
Weighted russian twist	45	50	55	60	65	70	75	75

CONDITIONING EXERCISES

BODY WEIGHT SQUAT

Purpose: To strengthen the quadriceps, hamstrings, hips, and glutes.

Procedure: Stand with feet slightly wider than shoulder-width apart, head up, chest out, and shoulders back. Slowly bend knees until legs form a 90-degree angle. Then slowly straighten to return to starting position.

Key points: Take a full range of motion. Keep weight back and knees behind your toes at all times.

SNATCH SQUAT

Purpose: Strengthens legs and shoulders.

Procedure: Stand with feet shoulder width apart. Hold bar over head with arms fully extended. Slowly bend at the hips, knees, and ankles until legs are at a 90 degree angle. Then straighten to return to starting position.

Key point: Concentrate on keeping arms locked out and bar slightly behind the head through the full range of motion.

FRONT SQUAT

Purpose: To strengthen the quadriceps, glutes, and hamstrings.

Procedure: Stand with feet slightly wider than shoulder-width apart, head up, chest out, and shoulders back. Hold bar across the front of shoulder with elbows high. Slowly bend knees, hips, and ankles until legs form a 90-degree angle. Then slowly straighten to return to starting position.

Key points: Take a full range of motion. Keep weight back and knees behind your toes at all times.

BACK SQUAT

Purpose: To strengthen the quadriceps, glutes, and hamstrings.

Procedure: Stand with feet slightly wider than shoulder-width apart, head up, chest out, and shoulders back. Position barbell behind neck. Slowly bend knees, hips, and ankles until legs form a 90-degree angle. Then straighten to return to starting position.

Key points: Take a full range of motion. Keep weight back and knees behind your toes at all times.

EXPLOSIVE BACK SQUAT

Purpose: To strengthen the quadriceps, glutes, and hamstrings.

Procedure: Stand with feet slightly wider than shoulder-width apart, head up, chest out, and shoulders back. Slowly bend knees, hips, and ankles until legs form a 90-degree angle. Finish by driving up on toes.

Key points: Take a full range of motion. Keep weight back and knees behind your toes at all times.

BODY WEIGHT LUNGE

Purpose: To strengthen the quadriceps, hamstrings, and glutes.

Procedure: Start with feet together about hip-width apart. Step forward with right foot so that right knee is bent 90 degrees and knee is above foot. Push off right foot and return to starting position.

Key points: Keep head up and shoulders back, and make sure knee doesn't extend past foot.

DUMBBELL LUNGE

Purpose: To strengthen the hamstrings and glutes.

Procedure: Start with feet together about hip-width apart. Hold dumbbells by sides. Step forward with right foot so that right knee is bent 90 degrees and knee is above foot. Push off right foot and return to starting position.

Key points: Take a full range of motion. Keep weight back and knees behind your toes at all times.

BARBELL LUNGE

Purpose: To strengthen the hamstrings and glutes.

Procedure: Start with feet together about hip-width apart. Position barbell across back of shoulders. Step forward with right foot so that right knee is bent 90 degrees and knee is above foot. Push off right foot and return to starting position.

Key points: Take a full range of motion. Keep weight back and knees behind your toes at all times.

PUSH-UP

Purpose: To strengthen the chest, shoulders, and triceps.

Procedure: Start facing down, supporting body weight with hands on floor. Hands should be under shoulders and feet slightly apart. Slowly bend arms to lower body toward floor then straighten arms to return to starting position.

Key points: Keep back straight and elbows close to the body. If regular push-ups are too difficult, change starting position to knees and hands instead.

BENCH PRESS

Purpose: To strengthen the chest, shoulders, and triceps.

Procedure: Lie on back on bench with feet flat on the floor. Grip bar with hands slightly wider than shoulder-width apart. Lower bar toward chest by bending elbows. Slowly straighten arms to return to starting position.

Key point: Bring bar back over the eyes at the top of each rep.

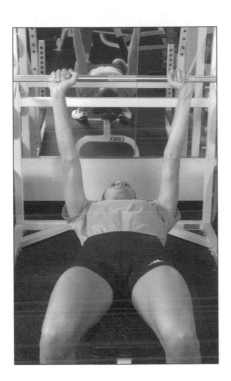 

INCLINE PRESS

Purpose: To strengthen the chest, shoulders, and triceps.

Procedure: Sit on incline bench and keep feet on the floor. Grasp bar with hands a little more than shoulder-width apart and lower bar toward chest by bending arms.

Key point: Bring bar back over the eyes at the top of each rep.

MILITARY PRESS

Purpose: To strengthen the shoulders.

Procedure: Sit on a bench with back support. Start with weight at the top of the chest and press above head.

Key point: Take a full range of motion.

PUSH PRESS

Purpose: To strengthen the shoulders.

Procedure: Start with weight at the top of the chest and quickly bend knees and drive bar overhead. This is similar to the military press but focuses more on legs.

Key point: Take a full range of motion.

HANG CLEAN

Purpose: To develop power in hips and legs.

Procedure: Stand and hold bar with overhand grip, hands slightly more than shoulder-width apart. Hold bar low with arms extended and feet hip-width apart. Lower the bar to knees by flexing at the hips, shoulders forward. Push hips forward and roll onto the balls of the feet while shrugging the shoulders. Bend elbows, pulling bar up, and move into a partial squat. Hold the bar on the front of the shoulders.

Key point: Concentrate on speed and quickness.

HANG SNATCH

Purpose: To develop power in the hips and legs.

Procedure: Use snatch grip and extend arms downward. Feet are hip-width apart. Lower the bar to knees by flexing at the hips; keep shoulders forward. Push hips forward and roll onto the balls of the feet while shrugging the shoulders. Bend elbows, pulling bar up and overhead with arms extended and knees bent.

Key point: Concentrate on speed and quickness.

ROMANIAN DEAD LIFT

Purpose: To strengthen the hamstrings and lower back.

Procedure: Stand with feet hip-width apart and knees slightly bent. Grasp bar with overhand grip and bar resting on thighs. Bend at the hips and lower the bar.

Key point: Concentrate on keeping the back flat and hips high at all times.

EXPLOSIVE ROMANIAN DEAD LIFT

Purpose: To strengthen the hamstrings and lower back.

Procedure: Stand with feet hip-width apart and knees slightly bent. Grasp bar with overhand grip and bar resting on thighs. Bend at the hips and lower the bar. Finish by driving up on the toes.

Key point: Concentrate on keeping the back flat and hips high at all times.

BODY WEIGHT REVERSED HYPEREXTENSION

Purpose: To strengthen the lower back.

Procedure: Lie face down on bench and anchor hands. Position hips on edge of bench so lower torso hangs over. Raise lower torso parallel to the floor..

Key points: Concentrate on keeping legs straight. Don't let lowet torso go higher than parallel.

PULL-UP

Purpose: To strengthen the lats and upper back muscles.

Procedure: Stand facing pull-up bar and grasp bar with hands shoulder-width apart. Pull up until the chin is level with the bar. Then slowly lower yourself to starting position.

Key points: Take a full range of motion: all the way up, all the way down.

LAT PULL-DOWN

Purpose: To strengthen the lats and upper back.

Procedure: Sit with thighs under pads. Grip bar with overhand grip, hands a little wider than shoulder-width apart. Pull bar down to collarbone.

Key points: Concentrate on keeping arms fully extended at top and squeezing shoulder blades together at bottom.

DUMBBELL BENT ROW

Purpose: To strengthen the lats and upper back.

Procedure: Grasp dumbbell with right hand. Support body weight with left hand and knee on bench. Right leg is straight and on the floor. Position dumbbell so that arm is straight and palm faces bench. Slowly pull dumbbell up by bending elbow. Then straighten arm to return to starting position.

Key point: Keep your back flat.

BENT ROW

Purpose: To strengthen the upper and lower back.

Procedure: Hold barbell with hands shoulder-width apart. Bend at the waist, holding back flat and parallel to the floor. Slowly pull the barbell up by bending elbow.

Key point: Concentrate on keeping the back flat and pulling shoulder blades together at top.

DUMBBELL PULLOVER

Purpose: To strengthen chest and lats.

Procedure: Lie on a bench with back support. Start with weight on the chest and extend arms up and over head.

Key points: Concentrate on keeping arms bent at all times. Take a full range of motion.

DIPS

Purpose: To strengthen the triceps, chest, and shoulders.

Procedure: Grasp handles with arms straight and body off floor. Bend knees and slowly bend your arms to lower yourself. Then straighten arms to starting position.

Key point: Take a full range of motion.

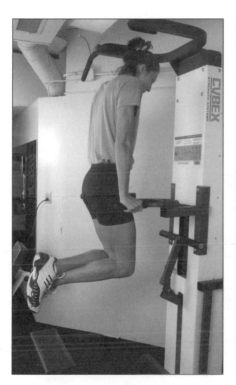

TRICEPS PUSH-DOWN

Purpose: To strengthen the triceps.

Procedure: Stand with feet shoulder-width apart and grasp bar with an overhand grip at chest level. Keeping elbows close to the body, push the bar straight down.

Key points: Keep elbows stationary and bend arms.

LYING TRICEPS

Purpose: To strengthen the triceps.

Procedure: Lie on back on bench and grasp bar with overhand grip, hands slightly less than shoulder-width apart. Slowly lower weight to forehead and then back to starting position.

Key point: Concentrate on keeping elbows stationary.

SHOULDER CIRCUIT

Purpose: To strengthen the shoulders.

Procedure: The circuit includes empty cans, Cuban press, and interior/exterior rotation.

Key points: Keep weights light. Concentrate on form and technique.

Empty cans

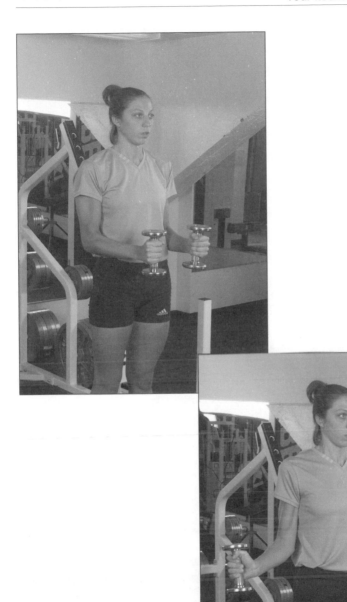

Interior/exterior rotation

Cuban press

CHAPTER 8

NUTRITIONAL SUPPORT FOR TRAINING AND PERFORMANCE

Volleyball athletes represent a select group of highly trained, physically fit people. Intense training programs geared toward maximizing their strength, power, endurance, and stamina make special demands on them as athletes. Rigorous training sessions and competitive events serve to challenge them and to develop their capacity of maximum physical performance.

Optimal nutrition is an integral part of peak performance and can enhance potential, just as an inadequate diet can limit potential for maximum performance.

What is optimal nutrition and how can you achieve it? It starts by sorting out sound advice from the many fad diets available today. Athletes have tried a multitude of ways to supplement their diets, including such things as bee pollen, liver extract, large doses of vitamins, and many other gimmicks. However, proper nutrition has the most influence on the performance of an athlete.

The relationship among carbohydrates, protein, and fat to the total amount of calories consumed daily is of major significance. The average American's diet consists of 30 percent carbohydrates, 30 percent protein, and 40 percent fat. As a volleyball athlete, your diet should be composed of 60 percent carbohydrates (40 percent or greater complex), 25 percent protein, and 15 percent fat. Unfortunately, most athletes' diets fall into the first category. Whether you are trying to gain or lose weight, this ratio is fitting for either. The only thing that changes is the total amount of calories you take in.

The food you consume falls into one of three categories previously mentioned: carbohydrates, proteins, and fats. Their caloric breakdown is as follows:

1 gram of carbohydrates = 4 calories

1 gram of protein = 4 calories

1 gram of fat = 9 calories

CALORIES

Athletes often overlook the stringent energy demands of daily training sessions. The amount of calories required is considerably more for the training and competing athlete than for the average person. But remember, those calories must be consumed in the proper percentage to the total daily intake.

If sufficient calories are not included in the diet, you will lose too much weight, you'll become fatigued more quickly, and your performance will diminish. These same symptoms will occur if you try too quickly to qualify for a certain weight class. If weight loss is desired, it should begin far in advance of the sport season and be accomplished gradually.

Here is a simple way to estimate your calorie needs and make sure you are getting enough calories:

Take your body weight and add a zero to it to get your basic resting metabolic estimate. Multiply that by 50 percent and add the two numbers together. The result is your caloric need for daily activities. Next, on the days you work out, add 15 calories per minute of exercise. This will give you your total caloric need.

Here is an example using a 180-pound athlete:

1. 180 and add a 0 = 1,800
2. 1,800 × .50 = 900

3. 1,800 + 900 = 2,700

4. 15 calories × 90 minutes of exercise = 1,350

5. 2,700 + 1,350 = total caloric need of 4,050 calories

With this example, 4,050 calories are needed to cover the athlete's caloric needs on workout days. But remember to keep your protein choices lean and stay within the 60-25-15 guidelines. Use the following chart to establish your own caloric needs:

Body weight (in pounds): _____; add a 0 = _____ (a)

(a) _____ × .50 = _____ (b)

(a) _____ + (b) _____ = _____ (c)

15 calories x ____ minutes of exercise = _____ (d)

(c) _____ + (d) _____ = total caloric need

CARBOHYDRATES

Athletes need more carbohydrates in their diets than the average person. Carbohydrates provide the primary source of fuel for exercising muscles. When a person eats carbohydrates in the form of sugar and starches, they are digested and circulate through the bloodstream as glucose—a simple sugar. If the glucose is not used immediately for energy, it goes into storage as glycogen in the liver and muscles.

When these glycogen stores are filled, the excess glucose is stored as fat. As exercise continues and more energy is needed, glycogen breaks down to release the glucose as fuel for the muscles. After a few hours of exercise, whether in training or in competition, the glycogen stores become low or depleted and exhaustion can occur quickly.

The best way to avoid this occurrence is to eat the right type of carbohydrates in their complex state. This will allow you to build up your glycogen stores rather than convert glucose, not only in the form of carbohydrate loading before competition, but as a way of life every day. Only carbohydrates can build up glycogen stores; protein, fat, vitamins, or minerals cannot.

Here are some examples of complex carbohydrates:

• Spaghetti, macaroni, or noodles
• Rice

- Potatoes (including yams)
- Stuffing
- Beans, lentils, or peas
- Bread, rolls, or bagels
- Pretzels, popcorn, or crackers
- Cereal (hot or cold)
- Muffins, corn bread, or banana bread
- Pancakes, waffles, or French toast
- Fruit
- Juice

Simple carbohydrates should be avoided. They include soft drinks, lemonade, Kool-Aid, candy, and typical junk food.

PROTEIN

The primary function of protein in the body is to build and repair tissue. Our bodies can only utilize a certain amount of protein, however. Since we have little capacity to store protein, any excess may be converted to fat if it is not burned.

The amount of protein you need is mainly determined by your body weight. Individual differences in metabolic rate must also be taken into account. Some nutritionists feel that high activity levels could also be a determinant, although the jury is still out on that point.

As a guideline, the average protein requirement is 0.8 to 1.2 grams per kilogram of body weight. One kilogram equals 2.2 pounds. If we figure a 180-pound athlete's protein requirement to be at 1.1 grams/kilo, his daily intake would be 90 grams per day. A typical can of tuna and a typical chicken breast each contains about 45 grams of protein, so it's easy to see how easily more than the average amount of protein can be consumed.

FAT

In addition to adequate amounts of carbohydrate and protein, you must also consume fat to complete a well-balanced diet. Dietary fat is a concentrated source of calories in our diets. Some fat is necessary to provide essential fatty acids and to transport certain vitamins. Stored fat is used as an energy source during activities lasting 20 to 30 minutes. Large amounts, however (as in the average diet), can prove to be very detrimental not only to appearance and health but also to athletic performance.

One thing to keep in mind about fat is that fat is fat. No matter how you look at it, it will always be metabolized in the same way. Sure, good fats (HDL) and bad fats (LDL) can have a positive or negative effect on longevity, but both types equal nine calories per gram. That means margarine has the same caloric expenditure rate as butter. Don't be fooled by television ads that claim otherwise.

Larry Rundle

Larry Rundle was a skinny, 6-foot-1 junior who had been cut from the Santa Monica City College volleyball team when he arrived at UCLA seeking a tryout. Rundle intended to transfer and was not about to give up on his dream of playing college volleyball. But he arrived at the Westwood campus with a clear picture in mind.

Rundle announced he was going to start for the Bruins his first season. "That was a mistake on their part," Rundle said of the coaching staff's decision at Santa Monica.

Rundle arrived at UCLA with full knowledge of the names of starters. Still, he insisted he would develop into the team's best outside hitter his first season. He then began a rigorous weight training program during the summer.

No American volleyball player worked harder than Rundle did that summer. And his work ethic paid off. Not only did he win a starting position at UCLA, he became a starter for the USA team. He was a first-team All-American as a junior and senior and captain of the U.S. Olympic team as a graduate student, leading the United States to its first Olympic victory over Russia. Rundle also played for the U.S. Pan-American and World Games teams and was a five-time most valuable player in the USA national championships. He also went on to win 13 pro beach tournaments.

Not bad for the junior college reject who went on to be enshrined in the UCLA Hall of Fame.

FAT STATISTICS

Item	Serving	Fat in grams
Coffee cake	1 piece	7
Croissant	1 medium	12
Pancake	1 medium	3.2
Snickers	1 bar	13.2
Raisin Bran	3/4 cup	0.7
Granola	3/4 cup	15.2
Cheddar cheese	1 ounce	9.4
Whopper with cheese	1	45
Quarter pounder with cheese	1	30.7
Taco Bell bean burrito	1	10.8
Wendy's triple burger	1	68.8
Tuna in water	1 can	1.7
Avocado	1 medium	30
Cantaloupe	1/2 melon	0.7
Rice (brown)	1/2 cup	0.6
Spaghetti with sauce	1 cup with 1/2 cup sauce	2.5
Baked potato with skin	1 medium	0.1
Bagel	1 medium	1.0

WATER

Athletes often neglect the water replacement. Just because you are not thirsty does not mean you are not dehydrated. Fluid loss is more rapid than most athletes realize and must be replaced as soon as possible. For competition, be completely hydrated the day before an event as well as immediately before, during, and after the event. One pint of water lost in the body equals one pound of body weight lost. As much as a 2 percent water loss in the body can result in a 19 percent decrease in performance.

An important point to remember is to drink *before* you are thirsty. If you wait until you are thirsty to drink, you're already dehydrated. As for sports drinks, you're better off choosing water instead. Too many flavored drinks are loaded with sugar and tend to stay in the stomach too long. If you do thirst for a sports drink, however, consume one after first having a drink of water.

EATING BEFORE AND AFTER EXERCISE

Athletes need sustained energy for long training sessions and competition. That requires proper eating beforehand. Before practice or games, athletes should consume light carbohydrates, such as fruits or toast without butter or preservatives. After practice or games, the best advice is to avoid overeating. Proteins are preferred.

USE COMMON SENSE

Most of what has been covered in this chapter probably is not new information, and it should come as no surprise that you probably know more about proper nutrition than you thought you did. You don't need to seek the advice of a nutritionist; just be disciplined about what you put in your mouth. Basically, you know how to eat right—now do it. That doesn't mean you must avoid fast food, either. Just follow a few guidelines.

- Burgers: Order a plain hamburger—broiled, if possible—with no cheese or mayonnaise. Order extra buns for added carbs. Throw away the bottom bun of a burger since it absorbs a lot of fat. Order lettuce, onion, and tomato. Add ketchup for flavor.

Proper nutrition will help a player be a stronger competitor.

- Pizza: Pizza is a better choice than a hamburger. Four slices of a cheese pizza with peppers, onions, mushrooms, and extra crust provide 50 percent of the calories as carbohydrates. Better yet, order spaghetti instead.

- Mexican food: Order bean dishes. Two or three tostadas are excellent sources of carbohydrates.

- Fried chicken: Remove all skin, which contains most of the fat. Order mashed potatoes without butter and minimal or no gravy. Eat rolls and biscuits with no butter. Order a vegetable that does not have any mayonnaise, such as green beans.

- Any fast food joint: Order a plain baked potato and add plenty of vegetables and a little bit of shredded cheese or bacon bits. Drink skim milk or fruit juice during breakfast hours. Eat fresh fruit from the salad bar.